SAN FRANCISCO AT YOUR FEET

SAN FRANCISCO AT YOUR FEET

The Great Walks in a Walker's Town
First Revised and Enlarged Edition

by

Margot Patterson Doss

Maps by Jan Hillcourt
Photos by John Whinham Doss, M.D.
Compiled from the *San Francisco Chronicle* Series

GROVE PRESS, INC.   NEW YORK

Copyright © 1964, Revised Edition © 1974 by Margot Patterson Doss

All Rights Reserved

Library of Congress Catalog Card Number: 73–21004
ISBN: 0–394–17863–7

Grove Press ISBN: 0–8021–0054–6

Second Printing

Manufactured in the United States of America
Distributed by Random House, Inc., New York

GROVE PRESS, INC., 53 East 11th Street,
New York, New York 10003

CONTENTS

ACKNOWLEDGMENTS

To the readers and walkers who wrote encouraging me; to the librarians, historians and octogenarians who shared their knowledge; to the architects, planners and redevelopers whose continuing charge it is to keep San Francisco livable and walkable; to *Chronicle* City Editor Abe Mellinkoff, because he is a city boy, and to *Chronicle* Sunday Editor Stanleigh Arnold, because he is not; to conservationist Hal Gilliam; to Grove Press Editor Don Allen who is more than willing to walk; and to my husband and four sons, a family ambulant beyond the call of duty, this book is dedicated with love and gratitude.

OLD TOWN

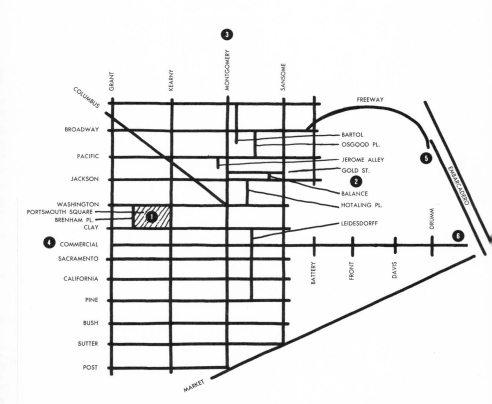

1 PORTSMOUTH SQUARE **2** BARBARY COAST

3 MONTGOMERY STREET **4** COMMERCIAL STREET

5 GOLDEN GATEWAY **6** EMBARCADERO CENTER

3

COLUMBUS
GRANT
KEARNY
MONTGOMERY
SANSOME

FREEWAY

BROADWAY
BARTOL
OSGOOD PL.

PACIFIC
JEROME ALLEY
GOLD ST.
5

JACKSON
2
BALANCE
HOTALING PL.

WASHINGTON
PORTSMOUTH SQUARE
BRENHAM PL.
CLAY
1
LEIDESDORFF

4 COMMERCIAL
6

SACRAMENTO

CALIFORNIA

BATTERY
FRONT
DAVIS
DRUMM
EMBARCADERO

PINE

BUSH

SUTTER

POST

MARKET

PORTSMOUTH SQUARE

Walking Time: Allow an hour to relax. **Distance:** Four city blocks. **Parking:** Down under. **Public Transportation:** Buses 15 or 55.

Among American cities, San Francisco is that rarity, an exciting town to walk. Indeed, as more people are discovering, now that walking as a noncompetitive sport is fashionable, it is the only way to truly know her.

The hasty motorist may taste, between his home and office, a tantalizing sample of her charms, but it is the man on foot who feasts on this rich and saucy city.

The fare could vary daily all his life. The city offers infinite choices: great walks and good walks, lusty walks and sad, hiker's walks, children's walks, sea walks, secret silent walks known only to the aficionado, and the noisy promenades of the gaudy, the greedy, the cheap, the gauche and the rest of us. Or if he chooses, a walker can go quietly through dell and highwater with the bird-watchers and still never leave the city.

As an opening excursion in San Francisco's manifold diversions, the novice walker might, for the sake of his calves, avoid both sand and peaks and begin his explorations where the city itself began, in Old Town.

"San Francisco has always been a city!" native sons sometimes boast, and by their definition, they are undeniably right. Before it became a city, however, San Francisco was for some eleven years the pueblo (village) of Yerba Buena (from the old place name *El Paraje de Yerba Buena*—the place of the good herb). It nestled between Broadway, Pine and Stockton Streets and the bay. Its waterfront has since become Montgomery Street and its heart was the plaza we now call Portsmouth Square.

Around Portsmouth Square on January 30, 1847, clustered twenty buildings. Four of them were shops, one was a hide ware-house, one a mule-powered gristmill, one a washhouse, two doubled as hotels and taprooms and one was an out-and-out saloon. The rest were homes. On the plaza itself was the most important build-ing in the village, the Customs House, which in its time was the local seat of two governments. It stood in the Brenham Place and Washington Street corner of the square (about opposite the site presently occupied by the excellent Nam Yuen and Sun Hung Hueng restaurants), and was built in 1844 on order of the Mexican governor, Jose Figueroa. Typical of municipal structures, it cost $2800, instead of the $800 allotted for it. This was a substantial price for an adobe building 56 feet long, 22½ feet wide, containing only four rooms. Outside were two long verandas and a tile roof. Many San Franciscans feel that the Customs House, our most significant historical taproot, should be reconstructed.

In 1962 Portsmouth Square, after many dowdy years, emerged from a face-lifting which included installing a garage in its depths. On the surface is one of the most usable small metropolitan parks in the world, notable especially for its children's play area, complete with a contemporary toy dragon to climb, and an outdoor game room for adults, removed from the children by the simple device of elevation. The walking in this neighborhood is enjoyable indeed. For historical appreciation, begin at the corner of Kearny and Clay Streets. When William Heath Davis stood here in 1833, this area was a potato patch, planted by Candelario Miramontes, who lived near the Presidio.

Two years later, on June 25, Capt. W. A. Richardson built Yerba Buena's first residence uphill on what is now Grant Avenue and the village was started. The following year neighbors arrived to build nearby. By the time Captain John B. Montgomery, commander of the American sloop of war, the *Portsmouth,* marched his marines up Clay Street to fly the American flag on the plaza in 1846, there was a fair crowd to watch.

The Marines had landed at a propitious time. Sam Brannan and two hundred or so Mormon followers arrived just 22 days later, looking for a place to settle. One report has it that when Brannan saw the flag he grumbled and swore, but he stayed. A year later there were 157 buildings around the plaza. One of them contained a printing press and one a school. It was Washington A. Bartlett, alcalde, as the mayors were then called, of the village who renamed it San Francisco. He did it to get the jump on another ambitious village now called Benicia at a time when settlers felt the town which bore the same name as the bay would be the one to prosper.

The Gold Rush and the forty-niners did the rest to make a city of San Francisco. Almost as soon as the words "Gold! Gold from the American River!" were shouted by Sam Brannan on the plaza, the transformation was underway.

Soon there were saloons, gambling houses, shops and hotels surrounding the square. Edward Bosqui, famous for his printing house, has recorded in his memoirs that once he climbed a ladder to the attic of the Old Customs House and found there the forgotten effects of officers killed at the 1846 Battle of San Pasqual.

It was in the Customs House, about 2 A.M. on the morning of June 1, 1851, that Bosqui awakened to see the Vigilantes hang thief John Jenkins from a beam at the south end of the building. Bosqui records that Sam Brannan honored the last request of Jenkins for a cigar by giving him his own to smoke. Brannan, in charge, then called for a mighty heave of the rope and Jenkins' cigar and life went out in the same puff. Legend says Brannan retrieved the cigar.

By 1879–80, when poet Robert Louis Stevenson arrived in San Francisco, the city had already expanded beyond Larkin Street, and there were Chinese children playing on Portsmouth Square as they do today. The marker given by Stevenson's friends and the tablet commemorating the square's historical flag raising are both there for the walker to discover. On the Washington Street perimeter, look also for the new Buddha's Universal Church. Cross the bridge to reach the Holiday Inn, a token Chinese cultural center, and in its side alley, Merchant Street, the famous Blue Fox restaurant continues to flourish, just across from what was once the old city morgue. Watch for historical markers throughout Old Town.

MONTGOMERY STREET

Walking Time: 30 minutes. Distance: 7 blocks. Clothes: Joe Magnin or Cable Car for rising young execs. Parking: Ghastly. Public Transportation: Bus 15.

If the legions of unquiet dead hover in the hectic air of late October, seeking out on All Hallow's Eve the ways they frequented in life, then surely the place to find them in San Francisco is lower Montgomery Street, counting house of the West, and without doubt, the grandest canyon in our jungle.

From a distance the bastions of the San Francisco financial district, which cluster about the meshwork of city lanes abutting

Montgomery near California, soar as part of that romantic sky-line which has been called, among other things, "an architectural zoo" and the "most beautiful in North America."

The scale was closer to the human dimension in 1850 when the mail steamer *Oregon* landed, bringing the official news that California had been admitted to the Union. Every banker, broker and merchant on the street closed shop to watch or march in celebration. The reviewing stand was at California and Montgomery and the favorite tune of the day was "Yankee Doodle."

Parades rarely come along Montgomery today, but the street, from Columbus to Market, is an interesting walk at any time. On weekdays Montgomery awakens before daybreak, when trading starts on the "big board" in New York and becomes a world with its own language, laws, traditions and superstitions. By 9 A.M. the "catastrophe of skyscrapers," as the world-famous architect Corbusier called them, absorbs enough brokers, bankers, insurance and clerical workers to populate Stockton. On Sundays it is an empty, echoing unroofed vault.

Compactness, always a fine feature of the financial district, makes it possible to see the big new buildings there without seven-league boots. San Francisco's first significant office building, commonly known as the "Monkey Block," stood for a hundred years on Montgomery at Washington. It was built in 1853 by "Old Brains," General Henry W. Halleck, on a foundation of redwood logs. The Transamerica pyramid, a spire in scale with the city's new tall skyline, now sits on the site, complete with mini-redwood grove.

Other significant buildings are farther along the street. One the walker will enjoy visiting is 420 Montgomery, where the Wells Fargo Bank has its history room. Here, as nowhere else in the city, the drama, humor, dignity, and sometimes all-too-human scale of Man's pursuit of money, is revealed. Wells Fargo also has a stunning 1877 photographic panorama of San Francisco lining the walls of its 14th floor executive suite. The photographer was Edward Muybridge, famous today as the father of the motion picture. It was he who photographed horses trotting so Leland Stanford could win a bet. In his own time Muybridge was well known for shooting his wife's lover in the cold white heat of premeditation. A jury acquitted him with the comment from its foreman, "Hell, we'd of done the same thing!"

Downtown offices are usually as inaccessible to the casual walker as the castle was for Kafka, but each year there is an office and industry tour sponsored by the auxiliary of the San Francisco Senior Center which magically opens flossy doors. This tour is worth watching for. It usually includes some fairly distinguished quarters, Wells Fargo's executive floor among them.

Some financial district buildings are visually exciting from the street. Look at the Bank of America building, the Crown Zellerbach Building, with its mall and witty carousel bank, the Industrial Indemnity Building, whose arches roof the sidewalk, to the delight of rainy day window-shoppers, San Francisco Federal Savings, which has an air curtain, and the Bethlehem and International Buildings. All of these have architectural concern for the eyeline as well as the skyline, a wonderfully human consideration common in great European cities, but in the past of wall-to-wall canyons, much lacking in ours. Such architectural enrichment could be a factor in saving cities as cultural centers.

Inside the new buildings the walker will encounter many other trends quickening. One is that industry has discovered the best employees, especially those whose work is dull, go to the firms which have the most pleasant surroundings. This has made it good business to provide generous space, imaginative color, good lighting, comfortable furnishings and elegant lounges unto the least of these. Calendar art and institutional blah are out. Gardens in the sky and fountains are in. Original art is now not only *de rigueur* in top-brass bailiwicks but also in corridors, cafeterias, waiting rooms and public lobbies. To hundreds of San Franciscans, reflecting the city's tradition of merry irreverence, the Mascharini bronze sculpture in the Crown Zellerbach lobby is already fondly known as "Olive Oyl," the great stone lump at the Bank of America mall as "the Bankers' Heart."

Montgomery Street had its share of stony hearts, among them financiers Charles Crocker, Collis Huntington, Mark Hopkins, James G. Fair, James C. Flood, "Lucky" Baldwin, Darius O. Mills, and Senator William Sharon. The stoniest that ever showed up on Montgomery was that of the city's first suicide, William Glen Rae, one-time factor of a Hudson Bay Company trading post at Montgomery and Commercial. When workmen were putting a sewer through this corner, they found Rae in a glass-covered coffin. His face was eerily identifiable through the oval glass. Some bystander admitted "Alas, poor Willie, I knew him, Horatio," or words to that effect.

Another Montgomery ghost one might encounter if given to extrasensory perception is banker Billy Ralston, who swam to his death at Aquatic Park in the days of rough-tough speculation in Comstock mining stocks, Black Friday and Asbury Harpending's great diamond hoax, all fantastic chapters in the city's business life.

History has continued to walk the street. The new Standard Oil Building, at 555 Market, is another museum free to the public. Until other Pacific ports can match it, anecdote for episode, and inch for thousand dollar running inch of front footage, San Francisco will continue to be *The City,* and the West Coast stronghold of a freedom sometimes called Capitalism.

GOLDEN GATEWAY AND EMBARCADERO PLAZA

Walking Time: Allow an hour. **Clothes:** Sophisticated. **Parking:** Ouch! **Public Transportation:** Union Street bus No. 41.

James Morris of *The Guardian,* in his excellent book "Cities," called San Francisco "the most lyrical city of the New World, one of the half dozen loveliest on earth . . . She is unique . . . She represents the civilization of North America at its most subtle and imaginative. She proves how gracefully Western man might have learnt to live, were it not for the preoccupations of war and power."

These are delicious words. But he also said: "I think we are watching the last years of San Francisco's prime." His primary reason was unlike that of most critics. It was that the City is becoming too much like other places, especially too much like other parts of the United States. "She is a little more tawdry than she used to be as the conformity of capitalism begins to swamp her . . ."

As in other places "we live in a rookery, and phoenixes are out of date."

This is a consideration the walker can take along in his mind while inspecting the redeveloped 44 acres now known as The Golden Gateway and Embarcadero Plaza. Well planned with buildings tall and short, much contemporary art, lively fountains, malls, and open spaces, it lies between Market Street and Broadway, close to the water but separated visually from it by the vise-like clutch of the doubledeck Embarcadero Freeway and actually by the *barrio* of traffic. Native sons recall the area as the old produce district, their grandparents, as Yerba Buena Cove where hundreds of sailing ships were abandoned in the Gold Rush of 1849.

A likely place to begin this walk is Sidney Walton Square, a contemporary Gramercy Park at Pacific and Front Streets. As you enter under the old brick arch that was once a part of Colombo Market, try to imagine the excitement that bubbled like champagne in the spring of 1960 when a design competition described as "San Francisco's $100 million contest" was judged by a top drawer, international architectural panel. There are still people who would like to have seen an inspired avant garde design by Jan Lubicz Nycz here, but the experts chose a plan submitted by the Perini Corporation, the joint efforts of Wurster, Bernardi and Emmons, Demars and Reay and Pietro Belluschi.

The sculpture in the park, Francois Stahly's "Fountain of the Four Seasons," is also a clock on which one can tell time by the rise and fall of water within an hour cycle. Climb the footbridge which leads to Buckalew House and to Whale Ship Plaza, a square surrounded by eleven small two-story townhouses, that give Golden Gateway airiness and perspective. Richard Henry Dana is the great stack of cookies that fronts on Battery Street, Macondray House, the blue tower. All have contemporary art worth seeking out. From Whale Ship Plaza, take the footbridge across Washington Street to the Alcoa Building, designed by Skidmore, Owings and Merrill. Only diehards insist that it looks like the box the Crown Zellerbach Building came in. The charming "Dandelion Fountain" of Robert Woodward is one of the delights of the second floor public park, which should lead down through trees between the freeway offramps toward the big blocky Vaillancourt Fountain, a symphony of water at play. From here it looks like the front yard of the great ziggurat that is the Hyatt Regency Hotel.

Another footbridge crosses Sacramento Street to reach One Embarcadero Center, the southernmost book in that tall row of books sans bookends. John Portman Associates were the architects of these buildings, and the late M. Justin Herman was the far-sighted man who would not let them block off Commercial Street's view to the Ferry Building. The phallic three-story stainless steel sculpture that pierces two levels of the plaza is not a smokestack. Willi Gutmann designed it.

Two blocks northeast is the misleadingly numbered Hyatt Regency, located at Market and Drumm Streets, but called Five Embarcadero Center. Elsewhere in San Francisco, with easy-to-remember logic, street numbering begins at the water or Market Street. The high hanging ball in the vast interior central court is "Eclipse" by Charles Perry. Steps at the far end lead directly to Embarcadero Plaza and its lively scene. Linger here awhile to reflect on Poet Philip Whalen's complaint that the United States really exports nothing but "downtown" and that it is possible to travel the world and never lose or escape it. And yet, and yet, viewing these towers from this mellow spot, one wonders perhaps if there is a fashionable phoenix after all.

BARBARY COAST

Walking Time: An evening. **Public Transportation:** Buses 15, 30 and 41. **Parking:** Be prepared to pay and pay and pay. **Clothes:** State your personality: gussy if you're making it a night on the town, underplayed if you're city-watching.

The bad Barbary Coast of the 1860's, which brought San Francisco international infamy just a little higher than the Devil's (a little lower than Port Said, Panama or Limehouse), was a lusty waterfront world that snoozed by day, boozed by night and hadn't heard of "split personality."

Today two different worlds of showmanship inhabit the sites or buildings of the old Barbary Coast. To get an insight into the picture, conjure out of memory a rinky-tink banjo thrumming loudly "Way out in San Francisco where the weather's fair, they got a dance out there, they call the Grizzly Bear," while a plaintive sea-worn voice moans, "I cover the waterfront," and a distant, well-disciplined piano politely interjects the strains of "Danse Macabre."

The piano speaks for Jackson Square, the present-day postwar and decorous day-world of decorators and their ancillaries. The

denizens of Jackson Square, who are ingenious with room dividers, *trompe-l'œil* and such, would like to close the storage-unit door on the skeleton sometimes called "Terrific Street."

The banjo speaks with a flourish for the night-world of amusing nostalgia, a refined but certainly lineal, descendant of the music halls and bottle gardens of the Barbary Coast. The night-world finds the Barbary Coast as subject matter as good, to use a line Ray Goman, of Goman's Gay Nineties used to sing, as "That old ace down in the hole."

This schism makes for good walking in the area bounded by Columbus, Broadway, Washington and Sansome, by day and by night, and certainly safer than in the times of planks, mud and cobblestones when the lady with the sea-worn voice, who is not to be confused with the pickpocket called "The Little Chicken," walked it.

General William Tecumseh (War is hell) Sherman himself, who once operated the bank at the corner of Montgomery and Jackson, couldn't get into Jackson Square shops without a decorator's license today, so if you plan to walk it by day, go on a guided tour or be content with window-shopping. First Historic District to be formally designated by the city, Jackson Square is a handsome anachronism.

For fun, take this walk at night, beginning at 10 P.M. when the contagious air of carnival is going full steam. To taste the heady thrill of danger that accompanied a visit to the Barbary Coast between 1850 and 1913, imagine you have walked up from the waterfront via Clark's Point on the Broadway or Pacific wharf, through the rookeries and rat-warrens where sailors were shanghaied, to Broadway and Osgood Place. A succession of clubs stood here, where John's Rendezvous was a long-time landmark.

On the San Francisco Committee of Vigilance map, dated 1851, this was the heart of Sydneytown, home of the Australian "ticket-of-leave" men who preferred an unknown frontier to the British penal colony on Van Dieman's Land. They also chose to open dance halls, groggeries and taverns with names like the Boar's Head, the Fierce Grizzly and the Goat & Compass which came to be known for bestial exhibitions. Women could be had there for a pinch of gold dust and the man who escaped without being drugged, slugged or robbed was lucky.

Osgood was Ohio Street in those days. Some expatriates from Tammany Hall inherited the neighborhood after the Vigilantes chased out the Sydney "ducks." It was during their period of domination in the 1860's that the Barbary Coast got its florid name. The cluster of houses on the west side of Osgood bear the unmistakable architectural stamp of the bawdy commerce of the early day "crib." Each streetside door leads to a court where steps give onto balcony-corridors lined with a pattern of door and window, door and window, door and window. Some of the cubicle walls have been knocked out and the buildings converted into apartments; one has a garden and a rear exit onto Bartol Place.

Peer over the fencing to see the brick wall of an earlier hotel that once occupied 50 Osgood. There are exits on five lower levels down the hill, one of which has a vaultlike wine cellar bolted with a two-foot lock and a 13-inch key, one of the city's safest blind tigers in Prohibition days. A more animated remnant of Barbary Coast history was the Gay Nineties pianist, "Professor" Elliston Ames, who pounded out "Show your lovin' beau just how to go to Buffalo, doin' the Grizzly Bear" at Tait's and the Techau Tavern, as well as in such Barbary Coast dancehalls as the Midway, Diana Hall and Purcell's.

The "blackouts" at Gay Nineties were like brief excerpts from the bawdy shows of Bottle Meier's, Bottle Koenig's and the Bella Union, which according to *The Programme* of September 1892, the *Variety* of its time, offered such distinguished titles as *Three Fast Men* and *The Tobacconist's Daughter*.

Walk down Osgood to Pacific, noting the indentation underfoot which is reputed to be a tunnel now cemented over. Johnny Leary's saloon once stood on the northeast corner, a hangout for the boys from Engine Company Number One, whose building across the street is now occupied by the Pomeroy Gallery. Kentucky Stables stood on the northwest corner. Solomon Levy, who "kept a clothing store away up on Pacific Street at 1 hundred and 54," was located two doors east of the firehouse. Other "thrift shops," as they are politely called today, and pawnbrokers stood on both sides of the street, one where the Barbary restaurant and bar is now. At the corner of Montgomery and Pacific you have reached the single block which was first called the Barbary Coast.

The block was also the southern perimeter of an area called the Devil's Acre. Battle Row bordered it on Kearny Street. Through World War II, Pacific had seen a succession of notorious dancehalls, deadfalls, melodeons and concert saloons. Today their names —Thalia, Midway, Moulin Rouge, Seattle Concert Hall, Spider Kelly's, "Nigger" Purcell's, Hippodrome—seem as colorful as the names of old sailing ships, but they were seedier than one can imagine from looking at the façades now. Number 555 has been given a gala carnival air by Alexander Girard's adroit use of color. Across the street at 560, the Showroom has a pair of celebrated bas-reliefs, done by the sculptor Arthur Putnam in the bawdy days. When first installed on the Hippodrome, the nymphs and satyrs were less modest.

Return to Montgomery Street and walk downhill toward Ernie's Restaurant, easily spotted by its old-fashioned canopy. Less easily spotted is the plaque on 809 Montgomery, which reads, "On this site the work of the Salvation Army on the Pacific Coast was started by Major Alfred Wells, July 22, 1883." The Major had his work cut out for him.

Saloon decor here dates from a period when you couldn't tell a saloon from a church without a psalter. Much paneling and the ornate stained-glass windows came from churches. Not so "Stella," the belly-breather painting behind one bar, which is reputed to have been at the 1915 Pan Pacific Exposition. Frank de Natale says, "Lights are what made her seem to breathe."

(This may be true of "Stella," but the belly-breather in The Tin Cup, a riverfront dive in Peoria, Illinois, which has hung there since Carrie Nation, an elderly, pre-Prohibition vandal, hacked the canvas, does it differently. A string attached to the back of the canvas and to the duckboards behind the bar makes the painting gasp when the barkeep walks to and fro.)

Turn into Gold Street, past the Four Monks vinegar works, to reach the art gallery, which stands on the site of the 1850–52 printing office of the *California Daily Balance,* edited first by Eugene Casserly and later by B. B. Buckelew. According to the California Historical Society, it was not this publication, but the ship *Balance* buried there which gave Balance Street its name.

The history of this site begins in 1844 when Benito Diaz built an adobe here, which he later sold to Alfred J. Ellis, who turned it into a grogshop and boarding house. Ellis had the misfortune to find a Russian sailor drowned in his twenty-three foot deep well. The Tea Garden Products Company later found the same well filled with molasses which had seeped in during the fire of '06, and sealed it with cement.

Walk through Balance to Jackson to see many famous old buildings, including the French Consulate at 432. On Hotaling Place, once Jones Alley, is the McGuire Furniture Company, formerly Hotaling Stables. Under Hotaling to a building owned by lawyer

Melvin Belli, at 458, runs a tunnel. Most stories of tunnels in San Francisco turn out to be apocryphal. This one is not. The entrance can be seen at Richard Lawson's, and was uncovered by engineer Frank Giuliano in 1959 when restoring the building. Farther along Hotaling is the cobble-faced Villa Taverna, once a stone-yard studio of sculptor Ruth Cravath and, in the twenties, of Diego Rivera.

Returning to the corner of Montgomery and Jackson, where a bridge once spanned Jackson Slough, or Laguna Salada, the walker can see through the basement windows, 494 Jackson, a wall incorporating a step-shaped bulkhead of the slough. The vault of the Lucas Turner Bank (see plaque) extends under the street at Murderer's Corner. Like almost every other building in Old Town, its history is long, variable, colorful and not always savory.

In retrospect, the walker will be surprised, not at the notoriety the Barbary Coast attained (enter to the tune of "The Grizzly Bear," one banjo playing, two miners drinking, three tough thugs, four Jack Tars, five gamblers dicing, six tootsies dancing, seven Sydney ducks and a politician in a top hat) but at the small amount of space in which it did it.

COMMERCIAL STREET

Walking Time: Allow half an hour. **Distance:** Nine city blocks. **Nearby Public Transportation:** California cable car, Sacramento bus 55 to Grant Avenue. Embarcadero bus 32 or choice of buses at Ferry Building at walk's end. **Clothes:** Anything suitable for the city. **Parking:** Nearly impossible around Chinatown.

The cradle of San Francisco, the source from which all urban blessings flowed in the city's formative years, is a narrow, little-known, nine-block byway called Commercial Street.

It is a lithograph of nineteenth-century buildings scaled to the human dimensions of a six-foot pioneer, raffish, smelly in places, vital and complicated with meaning for citywalkers. On it you may well meet a portly man of business with a Rolls Royce of his own, or a workman trundling an open barrow of salted fish. Both are part of the continuum of San Francisco's great banking, shipping, commodity, packing, produce and printing industries, which began humbly on or near Commercial Street when the lower half of it was the city's first important wharf.

Early maps show it as Long or Central Wharf, extending from Montgomery Street some 2,000 feet into the bay. Sansome was once a plank walk leading to it. In 1962 the lower half of Commercial Street began a return to oblivion via the Golden Gateway Redevelopment. The upper part still offers the walker a sense of historical perspective that is hard to come by this side of London.

The ideal time to begin this walk is late afternoon. The starting place is the Calle de la Fundacion, which is what Francisco de Haro called Grant Avenue in 1834 when he was alcalde of Yerba Buena. Not surprisingly, a plaque at 823 Grant announces that this site was the home of Capt. W. A. Richardson, first resident of the town. Commercial Street, however, had more to do with his next door neighbor, Jacob P. Leese, resident number two. It began as a backdoor footpath from Leese's home at Grant and Clay to a clapboard store he built in 1837 at Commercial and Montgomery.

Backdoor it remains for some of the buildings that front on Clay or Sacramento Streets. A notable example is the old U.S. Subtreasury building at 608 Commercial, the ground floor of construction begun in 1877. The rest was dynamited away in 1906.

Today Commercial slips unobtrusively out of Grant, across from the elegant Four Seas restaurant. Just down Commercial a step or two, watch for the establishment of the second oldest business in Chinatown, Mow Lee and Co., Grocers, who opened in 1856 nearby.

Grant is the highest point of Commercial and for years offered a pleasant view of the Ferry Building framed at the bay below, the only street other than Market that did so. Pick any name out of early San Francisco history—Little Pete the tong dong, the Comstock kings, Miss Piggott the crimp, Sam Brannan, General William Tecumseh Sherman, poet Bret Harte—all walked on Commercial and would feel at home on it today. The first block is nontourist Chinatown. Each successive block introduces knots of

CHINATOWN

1 GRANT AVENUE

2 ST. MARY'S SQUARE

3 THE LITTLE LANES OF CHINATOWN

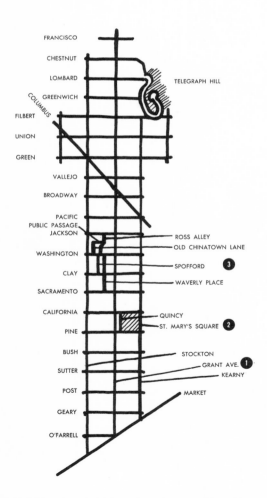

businesses, once ending with ship chandlers and waterfront dives, but now with Embarcadero Center.

Landmarks, plaques, quixotic signs, architectural oddities and minutiae for the history buff are everywhere at hand and underfoot. Set into the concrete you may see street names of brass, or old lavender and green glass, sun-discolored from original transparency.

The neglect which has preserved this old pickled-onion of a street is at an end. There are still vestiges of the unreconstructed roots of the business legacy that has nourished San Francisco— but walk it soon.

GRANT AVENUE

Walking Time: Two hours. **Distance:** 1.2 miles. **Parking:** Union Square garage. **Clothes:** Citified. **Caution:** Bring money.

Grant Avenue, the oldest street in San Francisco, has six separate worlds skewered on its short 1.2 mile length. A man could stride from its nether end at Market Street to its northern end at Francisco in a leisurely eye-filling hour. If he walked Grant Avenue daily for a lifetime, he would never truly know them all.

One is *le haut monde.* The many branches of New York shops in the section between Market and Bush have led one local joker to nickname it Fifth Avenue West.

Two worlds are *le haut goût.* Sang Yee Gah, to use the Chinatown name, is a gaudy, higgledy-piggledy quiddity transplanted from Canton, the street-level tourist trinket trail. Gee Gah is the warm walkup world of flats, family associations, fish on washlines, herbalists, rice and cha, cha, cha. What is cha, cha, cha? The agile teens of Du Pon Gai, as the Chinese call Grant Avenue, say it means tea for three. Chinese New Year, when the dragon comes out to play, is nationally known.

World four, Upper Grant Avenue, begins at Columbus. Once Bohemian, once Beat, it is once again off-beat North Beach, a pastiche of people, paint and pasta pots, bibelots, and an ocelot named Lancelot. The tribal festival of Upper Grant is a streetfair with mimes, rhymesters, folkniks, puppeteers, artists in nondress display, and dancing in the street.

Above Filbert, Grant turns into otherworldly Telegraph Hill, a latter-day Camelot that costs a lot.

The sixth world of Grant Avenue lives in history and in memory. This street began at a slightly more diagonal kilter, as Calle de la Fundacion, the first thoroughfare of the original Mexican pueblo. Captain Don William Antonio Richardson, the first inhabitant of Yerba Buena, laid it out in 1834. He chose it because Vancouver, Beechey and Dana had commended it in print as an anchorage. Spanish ships used to anchor inside Fort Point's cove.

At what is now 827 Grant, Richardson pitched a tent for his family on June 25, 1835. Three months later, after paying $25 for the first lot ever sold in what was to grow into the city of San Francisco, he built a house, lined it with the tent to better protect his wife, Doña María Antonía Martínez Richardson, and fenced it to protect his three small children from mountain lions and bears. The old 100-*vara* lots were 275 feet square (a *vara* was the length of a man's walking stick). Six hundred dollars a running foot is a bargain for land today on Grant Avenue.

David Brodie Torres, great-grandson of Richardson, who lived at 1251 Willard Avenue, owned the Mexican citizenship papers of his forebear. He could remember when his grandmother shrugged her shoulders because the gracious days had passed and said, "Let the gringos worry about that."

The gringos worried about truing up the Calle de la Fundacion, and when they did it, Lt. Washington A. Bartlett, then alcalde, named it for Capt. Samuel F. Du Pont, a friend, in much the same way mayors today dish out political plums.

Any site on Grant Avenue has a history of its own. The infamous Mammy Pleasant's boarding house, which offered interesting dishes including blondes, once stood at Dupont (as it came to be misspelled) and Washington. Norton I, Emperor of San Francisco and a favorite town character, died on the southwest corner of Dupont and California in front of the old First Congregational Church. In time commercial vice gave the street such a bawdy name merchants pleaded for a new *nom de bourse*.

Grant was granted. It has been a long time since a tipsy miner has spilled a poke of gold dust there, but Grant Avenue is as lively as any street in the city. It may be a shish kebab of truffles, bok choy, ravioli, baklava, cracked crab and the good herb, but a line from Bope Hope's theme song fits it: It may sometimes have been a headache, but it's never been a bore.

ST. MARY'S SQUARE

Distance: Two city blocks. **Walking Time:** With stops at Old St. Mary's and Kong Chow Temple, allow an hour. **Public Transportation:** California Street cable car. **Parking:** St. Mary's Square garage.

Not every street that disappears from a city is a loss.

A case in point is St. Mary's Alley, once the vile and squalid bailiwick of an international and mercenary stench of wenches. Thanks to the persistence of the Paulist fathers, whose injunction, "Son, observe the time and fly from evil," can still be seen under the clock across the street, this one-time slough of sin is now a public park. It is St. Mary's Square, an acceptably landscaped garage-roof and one of downtown San Francisco's most-used breathing spaces.

A walk around it samples several of the city's unique flavors. For historical perspective begin at the corner of California Street and Grant Avenue, one of our most admired, sketched and photographed confluences. To the rest of the world, the pagoda roofs, "dragon's glow" streetlamps, festoons of lanterns, cable car and outdoor telephone booth (whose calligraphy says "Electric Voice House") are unmistakably Chinatown. Dai Choong Low, or "Tower of the Big Bell," as the Chinese call Old St. Mary's Church, forms an agreeable architectural contrast, which is not surprising because the one-time cathedral got there first. Archbishop Joseph Sadoc Alemany dedicated it at midnight mass, Christmas 1854. Parishioners complained it was too far from town.

Tourists, aficionados of church decor and the faithful often find a quiet hour inside rewarding. The more secular can look south on Grant, imagining as they cross, a time when brothels mocked the masses en route en masse to Mass. Protests to city officials moved the lewd women off the dirt floors of Grant (then Dupont) and finally to the parallel backstreets of Quincy and St. Mary's Alley, but it took a shimmy along San Andreas fault to clean out the vixen warrens.

Turn east on California and walk downhill. On one side is the Hartford building. On the other the striking International Building designed by Anshen & Allen for American President Lines dominates the block with a foretaste of financial Montgomery Street beyond. It stands on Kearny where in 1850 the Old Plank Road, San Francisco's first highway, began. Unlike freeways today, the Plank Road had a destination and its route to Mission Dolores became Mission Street.

St. Mary's Square begins at Quincy and California. The casual observer might assume it to be the front yard of the International Building. It is not. The Japanese have a word for this use of a neighboring garden in an architect's plan. They call it *shakkei,* "borrowed scenery."

On the south side it also borrowed the picturesque Kong Chow Temple, which stood here a hundred years until it moved to a roof at Stockton and Clay Streets. Hou Wang, a monkey who made it to Heaven, and Kuan Kung, a general and patron of miners, are worshipped here.

The statue dominating St. Mary's Square, his back to Quincy Street, is Sun Yat Sen, as sculptor Beniamino Bufano conceived him, with a robe of stainless steel and head and hands of rose granite. In 1937, Lin Sen, then president of China, wrote the words at the base of the 12 foot statue: "Father of the Chinese Republic and First President . . . Champion of Democracy . . . Proponent of Peace and Friendship Among Nations." The statue looks toward a place where children play and old men dream in the sun.

THE LITTLE
LANES OF
CHINATOWN

Walking Time: At least an hour. **Distance:** 14 city blocks. **Parking:** Under St. Mary's Square or Portsmouth Square. **Public Transportation:** California Street cable car or Sacramento bus 55.

Eddying around busy Du Pon Gai, or Grant Avenue, San Francisco's oldest and possibly its most famous street, is a chain of little tributary lanes that visitors seldom see. Native San Franciscans, unless they grew up in Chinatown, rarely know them. The odds are that those who do made the discovery while jockeying for one of those pearls without price, a Chinatown parking place.

Compared to the lively inviting doors of Grant Avenue, the face these narrow streets present to the public is as reserved and noncommittal as rice. Yet most of the culturally sustaining facets of Dai Fow, the Chinese "big city" within the city of San Francisco, are to be found here and not in the brouhaha of the streets.

The walker who loves the byways will find a stroll around the lanes of Chinatown as exotic and mysterious as the smile of a girl behind a fan. The well-known restaurant of Johnny Kan on Grant, just off Sacramento, makes an excellent landmark to start from. History buffs will find the story of Chinese in America on Kan's third-floor banquet room walls.

Look downhill from Grant to 755 Sacramento at the Nom Ku elementary school which resembles a mandarin yamen, or courthouse. At 730 is the Chinese Chamber of Commerce where the dragon dwells when he is not out parading.

Uphill on Sacramento leads to Waverly Place, best known of the Chinatown side-streets. The YMCA, a church and the Salvation Army guard it, and its heart is the charming Chinese playground, which for many years contained a collection of fabulous kites, including a traditional rain kite made by Oliver Chang. The rain kite has eyes that whirl and a long tongue to tell the gods the people of earth are thirsty. No one has flown it recently.

Waverly has had several names in the past, among them Street of the T'ien Hou Temple. T'ien Hou, queen of heaven, protects walkers, travelers, sailors, actors and ladies of the evening and is still worshiped at 125 Waverly. Make sure the temple is open before you climb the four floors leading to it. Family associations and other temples on the lane are not open to the public.

At Clay Street go uphill to Spofford Alley, where a temple to Kwan Yin and a masonic lodge are located. Masonry, in one form or another, was known to the Chinese before Christian times, and Chee Kung Tong predates but is no relation to the western lodge. Radio station KLOK, which broadcasts in fifteen languages, is nearby. The walker who comes this way on a Saturday morning may also have his stroll livened by the music of the prize-winning girls' band from St. Mary's Catholic Chinese Center as they practice.

Cross Washington to Old Chinatown Lane to reach Chingwah Lee's Museum of Orientalia, a collection of art treasures which spans 5000 years and is not for sale. It is open to the public on Saturdays from 2 to 4 P.M. and holds open house during the Chinese New Year. If the next-door establishment's name, Aladdin's Cave, seems incongruous, be reassured by Scholar Lee, who says, "Aladdin was a Chinese boy who made good in Arabia."

The moon-gated house at the end was known as the "International Market" in the bad old days of singsong girl slaves. Look overhead for a house-to-house bridge, one of the last architectural remnants of the tong wars. At the end of the lane, turn right. This narrow passage, guaranteed to raise the hackles, leads to Ross Alley, where museum caliber antiques are to be found at Shang Min Lo Tin. The only pawnshop in Chinatown is also here. Ross ends at Jackson Street, where goldsmiths, bakers and sweetmeat dealers can be seen at work.

Half a block below Grant, the walker may pick up another chain of lanes where workday Chinatown keeps its accounts in calligraphy, ships dried fish, Mexican-canned abalone, fortune cookies and dresses all over the world with very little fanfare, nourishing the stream of "Old Gold Mountain," as San Francisco is called along Grant Avenue. The Chinese, who enjoy proverbs, have one that goes, "When you drink from the stream, remember the spring." In Chinatown, the little lanes are the spring.

DOWNTOWN

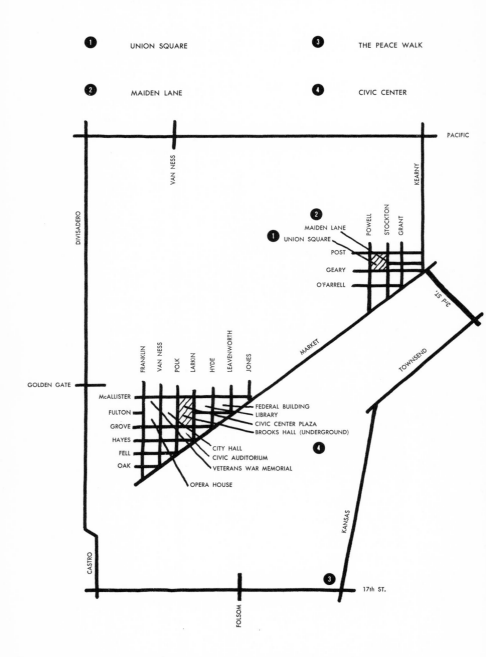

1 UNION SQUARE   **3** THE PEACE WALK

2 MAIDEN LANE   **4** CIVIC CENTER

PACIFIC

VAN NESS

KEARNY

DIVISADERO

POWELL
STOCKTON
GRANT

2 MAIDEN LANE
1 UNION SQUARE

POST

GEARY

O'FARRELL

3rd ST.

MARKET

TOWNSEND

FRANKLIN
VAN NESS
POLK
LARKIN
HYDE
LEAVENWORTH
JONES

GOLDEN GATE

McALLISTER

FULTON   FEDERAL BUILDING
   LIBRARY
GROVE   CIVIC CENTER PLAZA
   BROOKS HALL (UNDERGROUND)
HAYES   CITY HALL
FELL   CIVIC AUDITORIUM
OAK   VETERANS WAR MEMORIAL

OPERA HOUSE

4

KANSAS

CASTRO

3

17th ST.

FOLSOM

UNION SQUARE

Walking Time: Six minutes. Distance: One square block. Clothes: Your everyday mink. Parking: Down the rabbit hole. Transportation: All roads lead to Union Square.

No one has recorded whether there were any pigeons watching, but some 100 years ago, the placards in the public square on lower Geary street quoted Dan'l Webster: "The Union, the whole Union and nothing but the Union" and "Liberty and Union, Now and Forever, One and Inseparable," they said on May 11, 1861, during the biggest public-park pow-wow the city had seen. The message came across. San Francisco voted not to secede and Union Square got a name that stuck.

The placards in Union Square these days are more apt to quote Bertrand Russell. "March toward Sanity and Life," or "Hydrogen bombs are acts of aggression against mankind," they sometimes say, but the purpose is the same. For Union Square, in addition to being a garage roof, pigeon sanctuary, gerontological congress, floral showplace, stage prop for chic shops and hotels, breathing space and promenade, is also where the voice of the people is heard on the land.

No walk in town is so cosmopolitan as a stroll around and across the 2.6 acres of land bounded by Post, Geary, Powell and Stockton Streets. Its perimeter is Vanity Fair. Its center is Victory aloft. Its stable population includes chess players, shoeshine urchins, sailors on leave, footweary shoppers, newspaper readers, religious exhorters, sun worshipers, trysting lovers, crones, cronies, chronic crumb spreaders and a hazard of pigeons.

"Repent!" shouts a man hopping along the border of an elegant bed of violas. "You have nothing to lose but your soul." The lady in the be-daphned Dior suit, short-cutting from Magnin's, accepts the tract that is tendered, murmurs a polite, "Thank you," glances at "Warning, you are in great danger!" and never misses a step. As she passes, two sailors sprawled on a bench turn their heads simultaneously in an appreciative swivel. Sailors watch all the pigeons. A small boy puts a wooden box bearing the words "Shine 10 cents or 15 cents," in front of one sailor and smiles as a foot goes out automatically. A man in a wheelchair moves an ornately carved white queen on a chessboard, says, "Check!" and waits.

"Tucka-ta-coo. Look at the fool," say the pigeons, looking at you. "Look at the few! Look at the view!"

The ranter intends to say "condemnation" but his harangue comes out with an unintentional fillip. "You gotta get rid of the godamnation against your soul!" Sly smiles along the benches indicate listeners.

A young pigeon-feeder makes a sudden grab, launching a holocaust of flap, calms his catch, stuffs it into a pasteboard box and says to his friend: "Watch me get the brown one next time."

Across the plaza, he has been overheard. A pigeon-shaped man brushes a pigeon off his pigeon-splattered shoulder and bobbles, pigeon-like, toward the boy. "I hearda you!" he scolds, "You leave-a da brownie alone!" In a sudden movement he unlids the box, freeing four pigeons triumphantly.

"I suppose they all have psittacosis," one gray-suited, gray-haired professional man comments to his gray-suited, gray-templed companion as they walk, fending off flapping wings.

"Ornithosis."

"Too bad. So we can't say psittacines of San Francisco, unite! You have nothing to lose but your square." With one hand he shields his face. He holds out the other, palm up. His friend reaches into a side pocket, puts a quarter in the hand and asks, "Ever been in St. Peters in Rome?"

"Hellfire awaits you!" interjects the religious exhorter.

"Mate!" says the crippled chessplayer.

Two old people move to a sunnier bench.

A girl in sandals arrives with a placard. "The weapons of war must be abolished before they abolish us," it says, quoting John F. Kennedy. A crowd begins to gather.

This is Union Square. Just a short walk from corner to corner, but it measures the distance between the Kremlin and Washington. In an age overwhelmed with communication, it is still the only vox always open to all the populi of a democracy. Los Angeles and Chicago may refer to their areas of public assembly as "Bughouse Square" but they sell them short. The tradition is an old one, urbane and proud. It came to us from Hyde Park in London. By Forum. Out of Agora. Complete with pigeons.

MAIDEN LANE

Walking Time: Negligible. Distance: Two blocks. Parking: Sub-sub basement of Union Square. Available Public Transportation: Legion. Clothes: Chic. Add a hat on Monday if you're lunching at the St. Francis.

Maiden Lane, a chic two-block streak from Union Square to Kearny Street, is a promenade of the comfortably-buttered feminine upper-crustacean, which one disgruntled bill-paying paterfamilias has described as the "shortest distance between affluence and bankruptcy."

He may be right. This is a world of gifts from Helga Howie, shifts from Saks and Jax and Lanz and Ransohoffs; of pets from Ansel Robinson, jet reservations from Pan-Am, JAL, TWA; of cameras from Brooks and chimeras from more than one well-known portrait photographer.

Start this walk at either end between the elaborate candelabra one wag has described as belonging to the "nouveau richelieu period." Look down the little lane at the handsome plane trees set into the undulating curb, framed in red brick and matted with white dolomite chips. Don Clever and Welton Becket remodeled the street in 1958 to give it a saucy ambiance.

A sally down this elegant alley reveals that Matron Lane might be a more appropriate name. The citywatcher who avails himself of one of the thoughtfully placed benches on a shopping day will observe matrons archaic and matrons nubilic and matrons of resolute mien, each upholding San Francisco's reputation as a city of well-dressed women. Sporty country types sidle by on the bias. Prim high priestesses from the Junior League world of good works march, conspicuously white-gloved, into the furriers'. Models, overdressed and underfed, prance by like high-schooled horses. Stately clubwomen, boned and buttressed like ambulant churches, parade to the inaudible organ swell of "Pomp and Circumstance." Coveys of secretaries break cover for coffee. Clerks flit by hastily. Buyers stroll in pairs. The men are few.

A hundred years ago the men were many, for this was once notorious Morton Street, the bargain basement of the Barbary Coast. Until that sweeping house-cleaner, the fire of '06, wiped out the Morton Street cribs, prostitutes sat here in open windows, nude to the waist, and solicited passersby. A man could fondle one breast for a dime, or two for fifteen cents. More intimate services cost a quarter.

Iodoform Kate was the most infamous of Morton Street madams. She employed only redheads and bragged that her girls took on a hundred customers a night. The street must have been as crowded of an evening then as it is during the annual daffodil festival today. Old records fail to reveal whether the average of one murder per week could be chalked up to impatient miners tired of waiting in line.

Sin gave in around 1909. Merchants tried two new names, Union Square Avenue and later Manila Avenue, to wipe out the lurid past. Neither stuck and finally they borrowed the name of Maiden Lane from New York's former diamond market.

As you walk, notice number 140. Architecturally this is Maiden Lane's outstanding building. It was designed by Frank Lloyd Wright in 1949 and anticipates the controversial Guggenheim museum of New York in its circular ramp.

Culturally the most unusual shop is Philobiblion Bookstore, at number 50. Historically, the oldest business establishment is the pet store at number 135, founded in 1849. Owner Ansel Robinson has a picture hanging in the shop to prove that it stood at the corner of Washington and Cedar Streets, not on Morton in the gashy-flashy days. So far no one has dreamed for publication that she walked down Maiden Lane in her Maidenform bra, but there is a precedent for it.

PEACE WALK

Distance: 9½ miles. **Clothes:** Comfortable shoes, sweater. **Parking:** Best south of Market. **Public Transportation:** Market Street cars. **Caution:** Bring moral and physical stamina.

The fog that plagued San Francisco in the summer of 1962 filtered a muggy gray half-light on the corner of Kearny and Market Streets one Sunday morning as a cheerfully cynical and intense group of people gathered to begin a Hiroshima Commemorative Walk. Like similar groups in sixty American cities, they had outlined an area comparable in size to the epicenter created in 1945 when the first 20 kiloton atomic bomb dropped and they planned to walk its symbolic nine-mile perimeter.

"Wouldn't it be a gas if the South Pacific testing had diverted the thermal sources of the Japanese current?" asked a tweedy young man from Berkeley, regarding the sky.

"Or the Arctic shot started another ice age?" His companion countered, playing for fun the guessing game that is small talk among scientists.

"That's what the governor of Utah says about the milk." A young woman in an expensive imported handknit sweater said in a bantering voice. "Give it 60 days."

There was light laughter, not very hearty, along the forming double-column of people as they stood, receiving itinerary sheets or accepting signs imprinted, "Join Us. Hiroshima Commemorative Walk. Repose ye in peace," or blew up blue balloons stamped "Women for Peace. A World without War."

At 10:08 the column moved. They walked with ease and dignity, about 75 attractive, well-shorn, well-shod and well-dressed Americans. Among them were husbands and wives, many with young children by the hands; three, at the outset, pushing strollers, and two with babes in arms. There were older, silver-haired professorial types in sensible British walking shoes. There were students in cashmere sweaters under their leather-piped sports jackets. There was an aging golden girl, a California blonde in a wheat-colored suit and pale spike-heeled shoes. There was a man in a Coldstream Guards mustache; a woman in a fashionable tangerine-colored leather jacket, carrying a copy of *Four novels by Henry James;* a jolly-faced Oriental boy of 17 or so in a hooded gray sweatshirt. There were three well-trimmed beards, twelve business suits and no black "deathwish" leotards. They were what pollsters like to call "a representative cross-section of the population" who had somehow roused themselves out of the inertia and apathy that marks civilization's acceptance of nuclear contamination, and they were making a statement. It is a statement with which no one disagrees.

By the time the column rounded Portsmouth Square it had doubled in length, as it was to do over and over again throughout the day. Sports coats and sweaters began to come off as the walkers climbed Pacific Street. An elderly woman in front of the Ping Yuen apartments offered nuts to several of the children as they passed, and newsreel cameramen bobbed in and out among the cars, trying to capture action, character and setting, all together.

The signs borne overhead like standards looked like crosses from the rear and gave the procession an almost religious appearance as it passed, but this was no somber group.

"Fallout!" a student jokingly exclaimed as a public utility truck, washing salt-encrusted wires overhead, sprayed the line passing Pacific and Leavenworth.

"Spraying with Pure Water" was painted in yellow on the truck.

"That's better than pure Strontium 90," another walker suggested. The talk along the line, free-associating the news in the morning paper, touched in quick succession the contrasting concern of the State Health Department for poisoned oysters at Drake's Bay and its seeming unconcern with radioactivity in milk. In an objective voice someone remarked on the May 31, 1962, issue of the *New England Journal of Medicine,* which had reported on the relationship of fallout and leukemia.

The blonde in spike heels was gone by the time the column passed Oak on Divisadero Street. The strollers and light perambulators had increased and the sun was out.

Reactions of observers along the way varied from quizzical, if politely casual, observations in Pacific Heights, to bold curiosity in the Mission District. Along Pacific Avenue, heads turned briefly in the streets or near car doors. Along Castro and Seventeenth, windows were thrown open, people appeared on porches, some in shirtsleeves or undershirts, to watch as the procession passed.

On Seventeenth, a crowd of neatly clad teen-aged boys clapped when the double file had passed, more it seemed from embarrassment than any philosophical comprehension. Once the walkers were out of earshot, one boy raised a fist high in the air and shouted, without conviction, "We want war!" and a nervous ripple of laughter started, died and left the group momentarily silent.

Without further incident the line grew until it stretched three long blocks on garish Market Street in its last lap. More than 400 tired people sat down on the handsome exposed aggregate and concrete squares that pave Civic Center's promenade at 3:15 to hear three speakers.

One of them was Dr. Lucille Green who teaches at Oakland City College. She quoted the moving lines from poet Herman Hagedorn that begin, "The bomb that fell on Hiroshima fell on America, too," and introduced Mrs. Mildred Simon, an interior decorator who had visited Hiroshima, who described her impres-

sions in excruciating detail. If she had observed that the Golden
Gate Bridge, like the T-shaped bridge of Hiroshima that was the
target in 1945, lies in a funnel of hills where a river meets the sea,
plump and tempting for a bombsight, she did not comment on it.

"No More Hiroshimas" was worded on a sign above her head,
"No More Wars" on the sign in front of the impromptu speaker's
stand. A display labeled "H stands for Humanity" adorned one
of the Brooks Hall ventilators behind her and, from time to time,
buyers attending the Gift Show in the bomb-shelter downstairs
strolled around it, glanced briefly and hurried on.

Children played with their blue balloons in the Civic Center
fountain while their parents rested from the walk, a little-used
form of transportation which is being transmuted in our time into
a means of communication. It was a quiet crowd, only slightly
restive as the reports of letters from Japan and other peace-walking
groups grew longer and longer. To one side of the audience, Dr.
Monte Steadman, captain of the *Everyman II*, which had sailed
into the Johnson Island test zone, commented, "It may already be
too late."

Finally the message they had come to hear was delivered. Mrs.
Linus Pauling, wife of the Nobel prize winning scientist, introduced
as the person who has most "vigorously confronted the American
conscience on nuclear testing," declared: "Today the Soviet Union
has added to the pollution which has already reached dangerous
proportions in the world." And went on to ask, "What is going
to happen when China and Israel decide to test their bombs?"

The first thin fingers of fog were groping over City Hall's dome,
complete, unlike Hiroshima's. Overhead a jet roared, drowning
out part of her speech.

CIVIC
CENTER

San Francisco's City Hall calls to mind the old romance of Beauty and the Beast.

Whatever else it may be—symbol of local government, headquarters of the city's housekeeper, stronghold of the myth that says "you can't buck," and home of the 9-copy memo "buck-sheet"— City Hall is a beautiful statement. In the words civic leader Tom Magee used in 1909, farseeing San Franciscans intended Civic Center to say, "This is the modern city beautiful and the modern city useful."

Two international authorities, Christopher Tunnard and Henry Hope Reed, have called it, "The grandest Civic Center in the country." Another author, Mel Scott, described it as a physical demonstration "that a city is its people, that community character and love of place and faith in the future can transcend the greatest calamity, that the spirit is unquenchable . . ."

These are heady words. If they seem too sweet compared to the way three national magazines have described San Francisco as "a myth," "narcissistic," and "on the skids," come with open eyes and the scorecard to take a walk around Civic Center.

Begin at Fulton and Market, the focal point from which City Hall's elegant French Renaissance splendor (high score of 10 points on the plus side of the card) was designed to be viewed. Walk west on Fulton, which the first Civic Center plan of 1911 intended as a grassy tree-lined mall. (Mark the card −2 for the nonexistent mall. Now you know how to play this walking game so, as civic values always are, the points are up to you.)

CIVIC CENTER SCOREBOARD

VISUAL FEATURE	PLUS	MINUS
City Hall		
Nonexistent mall		
Handsome old Federal Building		
Lick Monument		
Three-fourths of a Library		
Brooks hole		
Temporary 100 N. Larkin Building		
Flagpoles		
Powerhouse smogstack		
Dull new Federal Building		
State Office Building		
Plaza and plaza fountain		
Civic Auditorium		
Gas station where office building should be		
View back at Market		
Rotunda, staircase and colonnade of City Hall		
Opera House		
Veterans' Memorial building		

The handsome old Federal Building, placing national close to local government, was designed in 1936 by Bakewell and Brown, the architects of City Hall. On the south side of the street the theater mimics the concave Federal Building setback in clever, high-flown contrast to the flyblown flytraps raveling out of Market.

Fulton widens pleasantly at Hyde. It takes a sharp eye to discern that the stately Library, designed by George Kelham in 1915, has a bite missing out of the northeast corner. Budget was the biter, as it was on Brooks hole, under the plaza.

Windy Civic Center Plaza has two "leaky" corners, to use a phrase planners invented to describe a breakdown in design continuity. Ugliest is the contemporary haybin at McAllister and Polk. In more gracious days stables and smithies were hid on back alleys. This corner belongs to the city and, according to Civic Center plans of 1911 and 1957, should be the site of an office building to house fire, water and civic service departments overflowing City Hall.

Oppressing the plaza as you walk west (dodging Old Faceful, the fountain that looks like a sewage aeration pond) is another monolithic monument to monumental government, the dull, too-tall block of the new Federal Building. In contrast, the State Office Building seems refreshing, but it isn't as handsome as the Civic Auditorium, the work of John G. Howard, Fred Meyer and John Reid, Jr., and built in 1913, contemporary with City Hall.

At City Hall entrance, look back toward Market Street which should be a commanding sweep. It is not. The flags are great when they are up. The signs are blatant. They're never down.

The dome, rotunda, staircase, colonnade and other details of City Hall are a joy forever. Once out the other door at the tragedy that is Van Ness, the walker meets a barricade, not a promenade. One must detour to cross and inspect the Opera House and Veterans' Building, mall and pretty golden picket wicket.

Tote up your own score to find out whether San Francisco is "on the skids." Seattle and Philadelphia (whose governmental homes excel) notwithstanding, Civic Center may be unfinished, but it is still a beauty. The beast, politics, could turn out to be a handsome prince after all. The scenery is appropriate to romance.

WATERFRONT

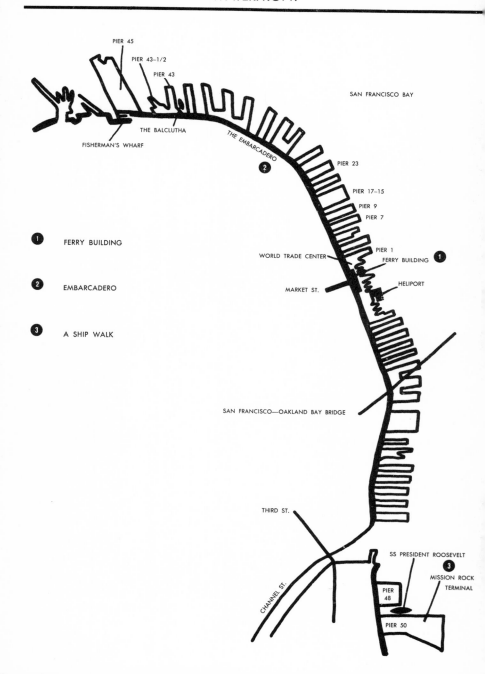

PIER 45

PIER 43-1/2

PIER 43

SAN FRANCISCO BAY

THE BALCLUTHA

THE EMBARCADERO

FISHERMAN'S WHARF

PIER 23

PIER 17-15

PIER 9

PIER 7

① FERRY BUILDING

WORLD TRADE CENTER

PIER 1

FERRY BUILDING **①**

MARKET ST.

HELIPORT

② EMBARCADERO

③ A SHIP WALK

SAN FRANCISCO—OAKLAND BAY BRIDGE

THIRD ST.

SS PRESIDENT ROOSEVELT

③

MISSION ROCK TERMINAL

CHANNEL ST.

PIER 48

PIER 50

FERRY BUILDING

Until the Embarcadero Freeway made a wallflower of her, the Ferry Building, our twinkling clock tower, water gate and romantic way station, was to San Francisco what the Statue of Liberty is to New York Harbor and the Palace of the Doges is to Venice—a symbolic and romantic belle of the bay.

To get some idea of her role, let imagination carry you back to 1914 when 100,000 commuters ebbed and flowed through the building every time the clock in the toylike, Giralda-inspired tower told 24 hours. The traffic was comparable at the time only to Charing Cross station in London. Old timetables list 170 daily arrivals and departures of ferry boats in the eight slips at the water's edge. Architect Arthur Paige Brown had reason to be proud of his arcaded terminal for it handled its crowds gracefully. So did the ferries. Unlike today's punitive bumper-to-bumper harassment, the daily commute could offer a restful interlude, a time of happy companionship, a fog-shrouded adventure, unexpected music, comedy, moonpaths and mystery. The fare was 10 cents.

When the bridges came, the party was over. But valiant is the word for the dear old Ferry Building, doing her best to carry on as only a lady can. Hospitable as the day she opened in 1898, she still offers to the walker at no charge a stimulating excursion, now through a smart mart and a recently renovated museum rather than the human comedy of a terminal. For those who "knew her when," it cannot escape being a sentimental journey.

Begin this walk at what was once the focal point of the city and now (after freeway) can be described as the bitter end of Market Street. The Sausalito Ferry leaves on the next pier west, alas. A wall now divides the building almost at dead center and prevents the right hand from knowing what the left is doing.

The left hand is doing famously. It shelters a kissin' cousin of the Chamber of Commerce called the World Trade Center. A ramp leads up beside a great Covarrubias mural, transplanted from the Golden Gate International Exposition of 1939 on Treasure Island.

The ramp gives access to two floors of indoor show windows whose displays often include motorized skis, Siamese paper temple-puppets and other commercial wonders of the exotic world of imports that funnels through the Port of San Francisco.

The right hand offers on weekdays a show of more enduring qualities. Approached through the great staircase to the nave are a handful of state agencies. Notable among them is the oldest tenant of the building, resident since 1896 before it was formally opened, the State Division of Mines. This wing, renovated since a man from Redding bought the famous panoramic relief map of California for $1, still has an excellent geology library, laboratories, and the mineralogical museum whose treasures would incite envy in King Solomon. It includes, among other wonders, a working miniature ore-stamping mill, an intricate glass model of the famous Guadalupe quicksilver mine and several safes full of gold nuggets.

Hidden under a stairway is the great mosaic seal of the State that thousands once walked over. The murderess Laura D. Fair and her victim, Alexander Crittenden, were not among them. The famous "Ferry Boat Murder" took place in 1870 aboard the *El Capitan* before the building was in use. The splendid water views once visible from every gate are now walled off, except from a few select offices and an exclusive club. The historic old Marine Exchange, created to report incoming ships, does not face the water. On the bay-side, except for BART ventilation tower, rents in the Ferry Building slips are showing.

WATER FRONT

Walking Time: Allow a morning. **Distance:** About two miles. **Parking:** Not bad on weekends. **Clothes:** Comfortable coat and shoes. **Public Transportation:** Embarcadero bus 32.

The working port of San Francisco is a compact, gat-toothed smile of piers whose upper lip is the broad airy road we call the Embarcadero.

There is nothing quite like a walk along the waterfront. The walker knows the horizon holds the Camelot city, the old, gold Teddy-bear hills of Contra Costa and Marin, the commanding bridges and the bay, but this is not what he looks at. The foreground has its own eye-compelling vitality, beautiful in contrasts. Cavernous pier sheds, mysterious when their doors are shut, may reveal imports from all the free world. Piggyback boxes wait by the sidewalk for the transport truck that will take them to Denver, Chicago and points east. Ranks of Volkswagens, tubs of soy and barrels of porcelain may stand by oil drums, bales labeled Karachi, sacks stamped Caracas or Callao. Sleek hulls loom great overhead. Fingerlift trucks scuttle, freight locomotives shuttle. Red stack tugs bob at anchor and the exotic, encircling bay laps cold and deep just beyond the bulkhead, within easy drowning distance.

Some fair day, to sample this strong fare, begin at the Ferry Building and walk north, past the odd-numbered piers, to Pier 43 where the Museum Ship *Balclutha* can reveal in her tween decks a history of our port's picturesque past, or Harbor Tours provide a bay voyage.

Ignore at the outset the sky-darkening freeway overhead. It ends fortunately at Broadway. Look bayward instead, where a Sausalito Ferry may slide from its nest on the old slips. A well-paved sidewalk takes up in front of Pier 1, home of the Bay and River Navigation Company. By the time you have passed the sign on the north side of Pier 7 which says, "Bulkhead Parking Reserved for Bar Pilots Only," and dodged a couple of barricades saying, "Warning! Cargo placed on both sides of sidewalk," you will begin to feel the excitement that permeates the Embarcadero.

Trucks, trains, ships and men at work demonstrate that this is a man's world. Women may walk here, especially if escorted, or if they mind their own business, striding along and speaking to no one. They'll be safe too, for ours is no longer a sinister port. But they will be stared at openly, admired if pretty, and possibly whistled at. The feminine walker should know this.

The shunting of cargo is a factory-like operation, efficient, impersonal, sometimes smelly with hides or diesel fumes, but it cannot hide the simple memory that the Embarcadero is our local road to romance. Here the great ships come and go, bearing the enticing intangible mystery of the unknown, the faraway. Some, like the *Oriana,* the *Spirit of London,* the *Oronsay,* carry people. They go outward bound with fanfare, champagne, announcements by name, like those in a royal court, and a flurry of paper streamers.

Some carry goods, like Isbrandtsen line's *Flying Enterprise,* famous for her heroic skipper, Captain Carlsen; or the *Jeppson Maersk,* or the *Kokusai Maru.* These may leave with a sea-muffled throb of engines and barely a toot of fare-thee-well. On a busy day the walker will see both kinds.

He will also see a well-known jazz joint, Pier 23, and the much loved Eagle Cafe, last vestige of a waterfront whose men remembered sailing ships and shared those memories over coffee here. Somtimes they still do. Another landmark, farther along on Pier 37, is the Crow's Nest, a schizophrenic restaurant, half simple, quiet and catering to longshoremen; half elegant, noisy and catering to architects and brokers.

But especially he will see gulls and ships. John Masefield wrote of both. Gulls, he said, incorporating an archaic Greek myth of Diomedes and the albatross into seafaring superstition, were the reincarnated souls of mariners. There is no record of a gull stopping at Pier 23 to ask for a double tot of rum. Of ships, he wrote, "You should have seen,/Man cannot tell to you/The beauty of the ships of that, my city."

A SHIP WALK	**Distance:** Cruise pros go 9 times around the deck daily. **Clothes:** Gala for bon voyage visits. **Parking:** Fair. **Public Transportation:** Buses 15 and 42.

San Francisco, one of the most beautiful natural harbors in the world, stretches from Lat. 37° 49′ N. by Long. 122° 25′ W. as far as her ships may roam. At any given time, seagoing segments of the city may be in Hong Kong, Honolulu, Acapulco, Yokahama, Bombay, Marseilles, Saigon, Sydney, Singapore or Port Said. It is not until you have seen homesick expatriates flock aboard in some foreign port that you realize how truly a ship is considered to be a splinter of the "home" named on her stern.

Great ships have always been part of the romance of the Embarcadero, as well they might be. Faraway places linger in each one. That sleek hull has nudged into piers fragrant with sisal, copra and frangipani, threaded through the sampans and junks of Oriental ports, outrun typhoons and basked under tropical skies. To walk the decks of an ocean steamer, even as she lies at anchor, is to live vicariously the exciting life of Conrad and Tomlinson, all in one heady breath.

The great ships of San Francisco are frequently open to the public on special occasions, such as Maritime Day, May 22, and usually on a ship's sailing day. American President Lines, the largest San Francisco-based shipowner, for example, will schedule guided tours of its ships when they are in port, for school classes, church and civic groups. So popular are these ship walks that appointments are booked months in advance. But on a sailing day, by picking up a pass ahead of time, almost anyone may go aboard a ship before she casts off from the pier, especially if it is to wish a friend bon voyage.

Twelve passengers only are permitted on the "tramp steamers"— the cargoliners, seamasters, mariners and sea racers that bear the names of U. S. presidents. (As a union member I hate to admit that the big luxe liners like the SS *President Roosevelt* have been priced out of existence, alas, by union wages that failed to reckon with the competition of foreign bottoms.) Containers of cargo, big as a truck, take up the rest of the space in these long slim 550′ to 650′ hulls. One of the great anomalies is that these seagoing warehouses are luxury craft with passenger appointments as elegant as any hotel, each a little like a palace set down in a corporation yard.

Come with me in memory for a "turn around the decks", as cruise pros say, and hope that you will be lucky enough to take this walk sometime when the *President Fillmore* or one of her sister ships is in her home port next time. The walk begins at Pier 80, at the foot of Army Street, in a cavernous cargo shed sometimes set about with jute bags of cinnamon bark and cocoa nut or boxes of table china, but more often with shiny, anonymous metal cargo containers stacked beautifully in patterns like children's blocks arranged by a giant. No lobby, the gangway (a far cry from the canopy, ornate as the Opera House and set among balloons, officials and porters that once led up to the luxury liners), may accommodate stowage alternately with passengers.

Reach the cabin deck, step through a passage and, miraculously, the factory ambiance is shed instantly. The floors are hand-pegged teak random planking or lush, handcarved broadloom carpeting, some of it patterned like an impression of seawaves.

Turn aft to find a main lounge, library, a cardroom that doubles as a bar (as in a private club, each passenger has his own liquor locker) and deck space for outdoor shuffleboard.

Here you really get the feeling of a ship. The lifeboats are snugged into their davits, brass fittings gleam against the tung-soaked teak railings, and white ventilators jut out inexplicably. Look up amidships to see the eagle that identifies the "Fillmore" as an APL ship, and climb up to it if you will, for that central stack is an observation platform in disguise. The real stacks flank it. Only the radar post goes higher. Look forward toward the bow to see the bridge where the captain, as James Morris once wrote, "stands godlike in his power." Aboard the *Fillmore,* Captain Robert T. Kenney looks rather more suave, but the skipper of the *President Tyler,* Captain Lee Jewett, lanky as Long John Silver, arms tattooed, face weatherworn, walks with the rolling gait of the classic seafarer. Hollywood couldn't have done a better job of typecasting.

From the lounge, go below one deck by way of the impressive teak railed staircase to reach the dining room (which would have been called the saloon aboard a sailing ship), an intimate space where there are tables for passengers and the ship's officers who dine with them.

Then swing back topside to seek out the marine veranda, where deck chairs await, their knees folded like a row of grasshoppers, or twelve comic husbands waiting for a vacuum cleaner to sweep underfoot. This is where the gossips gather, friendships, suntans and romances begin and frazzled nerves untwist and restore themselves.

Our superficial walk can show you how the ship looks inside, but nothing short of a real trip can ever teach you the bunk-rocking pitch, dip and roll of the sea, the relaxation possible so far from traffic and telephones, the healing anodyne of long days with no demands and the breathtaking surprise of your first glimpse of a flight of flying fish. To find these you must take the cruise. The waiting list forms uptown at the new International Building on St. Mary's Square.

NOB HILL

1   JOICE STREET   3   GRACE CATHEDRAL CLOSE

2   HUNTINGTON SQUARE   4   PRIEST STREET

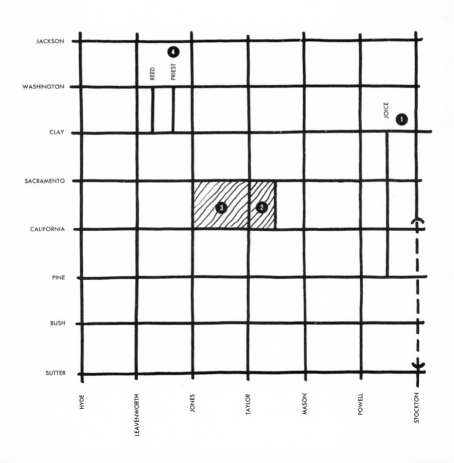

NOB HILL

Walking Time: All your life. **Distance:** As far as democracy will let you go. **Clothes:** Sable, Savile Row, or forget it. **Parking:** That's the chauffeur's job. **Public Transportation:** The Big Four used the cable cars.

Nob Hill, a legacy from the nabobs who out-Horatioed Alger to the expense-account princes of our Affluent Age, is synonymous in San Francisco with rank, swank and status. Its crest is an altar of the American cult called business to the goddess, sweet Success. It is also our best-known hill and pleasant indeed to walk about.

For Nob is a man's hill, with power in the air, privilege in a stair and prestige in a chair. Its square heart is a stolid old brownstone mansion built in 1886 by bonanza king James C. Flood to prove he'd made the grade from corned beef to caviar. Its periphery is a wreath of establishments that could be grouped under one word, singular.

Begin this walk, as history did in 1856, at the corner of California and Powell Streets, the crossroads of two cable cars. Here, on the site of the Fairmont Hotel, Dr. Arthur Hayne built a home for his bride, actress Julia Dean, after cutting a trail uphill through chaparral. Men of wealth soon followed his trail. Within a few years Leland Stanford, Mark Hopkins, Charles Crocker, E. J. (Lucky) Baldwin had all constructed elaborate palaces. The steep block that goes uphill on California to Mason Street will show you why they waited for the arrival of the California Street cable car to build them. Horses found the pull as steep as the walker will.

All the vainglorious display, except the Flood mansion, now an exclusive men's club, went down in the '06 fire. The foundations of the palace James G. (Bonanza Jim) Fair had planned to build to outshine all the rest were later incorporated into the Fairmont Hotel. "Tessie" Fair Oelrichs built the hotel in 1906 and rebuilt it in 1907 to immortalize her father, and it is still the grandest tiger in the jungle.

Across the street, the Mark Hopkins mansion was first replaced by an Institute of Art, which now lives on nearby Russian Hill, and later by the hotel whose tower view tourists treasure. Walk around the Pacific Union Club to reach Huntington Park, once the site of another millionaire's showplace, and now a much-used breathing spot. Grace Cathedral close, across the street, a gift from the Crocker family, replaced the redwood homes that once stood here. The Masonic Temple, whose stark white seems paradoxical next to the Gothic of the Cathedral and the Edwardian architecture of the Flood mansion, is on the sites of more bygone glory, the homes of A. N. Towne (whose portals are now a garden ornament in Golden Gate Park), Robert Sherwood and George Whittell. All, all are gone, the old familiar houses. Today Nob Hill has halls, church, lodge, club, apartment buildings and hotels, and Lo! it equals the pomp of yesteryear.

JOICE STREET

Distance: Three city blocks. **Walking Time:** Six to ten minutes. **Clothes:** Last year's suit. **Parking:** None. **Public Transportation:** Powell Street cable car going. California Street cable car returning.

Threading the lee of Ern Hill, Fern Hill, or the Hill of Golden Promise, as Nob Hill was known for the first twenty years of its civic existence, is an obscure three-block-long shelf called Joice Street, where Time, like any other climber, stopped to take a deep breath before going on to the top.

It is a modest street, uncommercial and almost unknown. For 120 years the frantic life of downtown San Francisco has swirled about it madly. In all that time the changes have been so reassuringly few that any walker can retrieve the threads of continuity that link the surreal present with the more civilized recent past.

Begin this walk in Chinatown on Clay Street below Powell, across from the Commodore Stockton grammar school. It was down Clay Street at 5 A.M., August 2, 1873, that Andrew S. Hallidie, his partners and a gripman named Jimmie made the historic test run in the first cable car ever built. By the time they reached Joice Street, they were in a dense fogbank, tense and eager to stop rolling. The trip was a success. The Clay Street Railroad Company, since absorbed by the Muni, had launched what has become San Francisco's best-loved anachronism.

Look down Joice Street before you begin to walk it. It has a noticeable backdoor ubiety, narrow and appropriate to service entrances and stable-door accesses. San Francisco's first exclusive residential section grew up just downhill on Stockton Street. Children who walked to Dr. Ver Mehr's Episcopal parish school along this lane in 1850 must have watched with excitement as "Gold was found" (according to Soulé, Gihon and Nisbet in *The Annals of San Francisco*) in "the sand taken from a great depth in sinking wells in Stockton Street."

Two years later, Soulé, *et al.*, record, "Stockton Street was being ornamented with many handsome brick tenements, which were intended for the private residences of some of the wealthier citizens." One of them, 806 Stockton, was the home of Francis L. A. Pioche, pioneer financier and bon vivant credited with giving to San Francisco an appreciation of fine food. He imported many French chefs and a cargo of vintage wines. His stables fronted Joice Street, as several carports and tree-shaded parking areas do today.

One parking lot formerly held the refuge house of the Presbyterian Chinese Mission, long a sanctuary for broken lilies from old Canton. Cameron House, at the southeast corner of Sacramento and Joice, is named in honor of Donaldina Cameron, whom the Chinese called "Lo Mo," the mother, for her lifetime of work freeing singsong slave girls. Her long-time assistant, Lorna Logan, is now social work director and reports that the last slave came to the community center in 1934. Go inside to see beautiful old carved cornices, calligraphy and paintings.

As you cross Sacramento, look downhill toward the Stockton Street tunnel where a bucolic cottage hides on the cliff face. A great swing hangs from its wonderful front-yard willow tree, one of the most unexpected visual delights to be found in this part of the city.

At California before you reach the corner, look for the formal little garden that gives a lift to this city eyeline. Across broad California Street, which led grandly to the great mansions of the "nabobs" who gave Nob Hill its name, Joice Street eases along quietly for another half block, then drops precipitously to end at Pine in a garden-like oasis with another surprise. There in the heart of the city, shyly hidden in the shrubs that line the steps, is a well-tended wayside shrine. It was built, with love and devotion, by Ronald Telfer, who lived on Joice Street for many years, and it is still tended by friends, relatives and admirers, long after his death.

GRACE CATHEDRAL CLOSE

Walking Time: Six minutes. Allow one to three hours to explore the Cathedral. **Clothes:** Ladies will be more comfortable in hat and gloves. **Parking:** Masonic Temple garage. **Public Transportation:** California cable car or Sacramento bus 55. **Children:** Tots may be parked for most services at the nursery in stone building north of the bell towers.

When the stunning tintinnabulation of "Adeste Fideles" rings out loud and clear over Nob Hill on the Grace Cathedral carillon, Scrooges, sourpusses, overworked salespeople and atomic scare-mongers to the contrary notwithstanding, to anyone in earshot, Christmas once again takes on its historical dimension as the hope of the world.

"O' come all ye faithful," the bells sing, and the rush, bustle, spangles, tinsel and tawdriness of our affluent commerciality diminish like the piping of a penny whistle. This, the mind says, is the real thing, the world series of religion, Christendom's annual big birthday party, miraculous and nearly two thousand years old. Joy to the world. Unto us a child is given.

Whatever his denominational persuasion, the walker who explores Grace Cathedral close, which is the square block bounded by California, Sacramento, Taylor and Jones Streets, will find it alive with three dominant phenomena of our times: The flurry of building construction, the resurgence of interest in religion, and the fearless, forthright Episcopal Bishop of California, not, of course, listed in their ultimate order of importance.

Begin this walk at the corner of Taylor and California, as early as you please, for life at Grace Cathedral takes hold of the wings of the morning while most of us are slugabed. At the outset, examine the Ghiberti gates which stand between the twin to Coulson bell tower and the extension of the Cathedral nave. The munificence of many citizens, among them W. W. Crocker, whose family also gave the land on which the Cathedral stands, makes this construction possible. Inside the north "Singing Tower" are 43 bells with names like Sympathy, Isaiah and Loving Kindness. Richard Purvis was the genius who first brought them to exuberance, sometimes on such secular occasions as the winning of a baseball pennant.

The soaring cathedral beckons the beholder with a taste for grandeur. Resist for the present, if you can, and walk along Taylor Street instead. On one side is Huntington Park, whose fountain is a replica of the Tartarughe fountain in Rome. Diana Crocker can recall when it stood on her grandfather's estate, now the Burlingame Country Club, and had turtles in the basin. On the other side are Cathedral and Diocesan houses, elegant office buildings of the church, both reminiscent of the seventeeth-century Mompesson house of Salisbury Cathedral close. The juxtaposition of close, castle-like hotels, exclusive gentlemen's club and the park has led one wit to call this area "that corner of San Francisco which is forever England."

Bear left uphill along Sacramento, past the wrought-iron gate. This was once the site of a 40-foot spite fence to shut out a Chinese neighbor. The playing field at the northwest corner belongs to the Cathedral School for Boys and tops a contemporary school building. Pause at Jones before turning south and look back to see one of our most civilized cityscapes.

From Jones, east on California will take you to the main entrance of the Cathedral. For many years the cornerstone, now incorporated into the new construction, stood here beside the steps, a monument to the impatience of Bishop William F. Nichols, who laid it in a drenching rain in 1910 before blueprints were drawn.

Inside the cathedral is many splendored. It is also busy. On Christmas Eve, it is busiest of all, when strangers, the weary, and those whom Dean C. Julian Bartlett calls the unchurched are welcomed in resonant tones in honor of a Child born in a stable.

PRIEST STREET

Walking Time: Six minutes. **Available Public Transportation:** Powell-Hyde cable cars to Jones Street. **Parking:** None. **Suitable Clothing:** Urban tweeds. **Distance:** A city block in space, one hundred years in time.

The little lanes of Nob Hill have their own distinctive flavors, but few have such bittersweet sadness as the one which slips modestly down from the crest to emerge next to 1333 Washington Street.

"End Priest" its sign says cryptically. More than one passenger on the Hyde Street cable car must wonder where Priest begins. It begins, as far as one can tell from street signs, at the place of its ending. If relevance could alter street signs, it might say instead "Begin Paradox." Here, as nowhere else in San Francisco, yesterday has been disrobed and stands, all moss and innocence, revealed before a thousand lenses of tomorrow.

For the walker who prides himself on savoir faire and objectivity an excursion up the steps of Priest Street will be enlightening. Luxurious ivy banks the right side of the steps. About fifty feet uphill the steps level out in front of the first of five houses on the street. All but one are modest, unassuming flats whose rents have long been within reach of a nurse, a stenographer, or a young columnist. None is new, and one, a brown-shingled classic, has mellowed through fifty rainy seasons or more. In contrast, the gardens seem discouragingly raw, and so they are. Not long ago, slides from undermining bulldozers toppled the old trees which had given this lane rustic charm, a human dimension, and above all, safely shared privacy.

The sense of inappropriate newness of the plantings will hit the walker at about the same time he becomes aware of being watched. On the left, or east, side of the street, stacked like an indecently tall club sandwich of glass from which wistful vestigial balcony gardens ravel a little greenery, like tired lettuce, is Nob Hill's new landmark, the slab of community apartments which has replaced a reservoir. Like a vertical Terra Linda, the picture windows are sitting on each other's eyebrows.

"Oh yes, I have to keep the blinds three-quarters drawn." One Priest Street resident of forty years says.

Another, Mrs. Therese Dinneen, a merry-eyed Frenchwoman who built three of the Priest Street houses and owns all but one, has spent fifty years here. "I don't resent the new building," she says: "It's their land, but the street doesn't seem to have the country-like setting anymore, and of course, we have lost the view." Her view west covers a 180° arc, and to protect it, she has had to buy two lots behind her on the adjoining lane, Reed Street.

Both Reed and Priest end abruptly in a vacant lot whose steep sides are banked with trees, but passage from one to the other is difficult. Leashed dogs from nearby apartments, whose inaccessible plantings have been designed to discourage them, find this little plot of earth a haven. It stands on yesterday's side of the street.

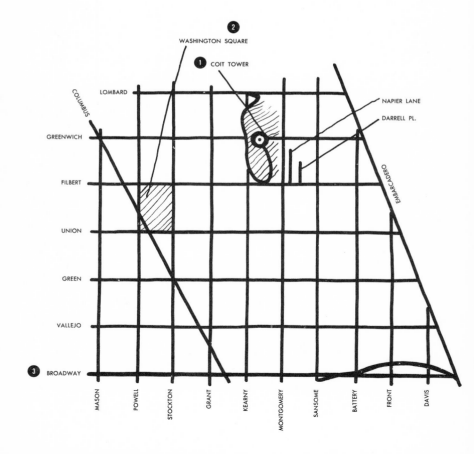

1. COIT TOWER

2. WASHINGTON SQUARE

3. BROADWAY

TELEGRAPH HILL

Walking Time: Allow a morning.
Nearby Public Transportation:
Coit bus 39 to the top of the hill.
Evans bus 42 on Sansome Street.
Parking: Difficult. **Clothing:** Flat-
heeled shoes. Be prepared to shed
your jacket.

Among San Francisco hills, Telegraph is the Marlene Dietrich, with a trench coat of trees tossed over her sophisticated shoulders. She wears, with great insouciance, tattered underskirts, a continental strand of bistros on one ankle, and a chain of working piers on the other. Day and night tourists pay tribute to the geographical elegance of the little hill top the Spaniards called Loma Alta, to Lillie Coit's firehose-nozzle tower, to the Christopher Columbus monument and to the re-established semaphore. Some learn the hill was the location of the first commercial telegraph station. A few pause to see what the boys in the back streets are having.

The boys and the girls on the back streets are having a ball. The living is easy, if expensive, in this aerie of upper Bohemia. It ranges from informal, first name, hut-to-hut talk on Catfish Row, as Napier Lane is sometimes called, to the chic-freeze of inter-nationally correct addresses nearby.

The walker who is game for surprises will find them on Tele-graph's steep slope. One word of caution: Walk it first by day. The labyrinth of lanes is so intricate postman Don Lam, who grew up in nearby Chinatown, admits he got lost when first delivering mail on the hill. No one is lost long. The landmarks are too famous. To begin exploring, find the Greenwich Street sign at the east rim of Coit Tower's parking circle. Here red-brick steps lead down into a hushed tunnel of mounded shrubs.

After a bobby-pin curve, the steps pause at a lane. Walk left toward the villa of Doctors Bill and Jep Hunter (marked by a guruda on the door), once the residence of well-known editor Paul Smith. For a closeup of the cliff dynamited into the hill by brothers Harry N. and George F. Gray, look through the old Spanish wrought-iron gate that leads to decorator Anthony Hail's grotto-like studio. Whole lots toppled because of the six selfish years of blasting that left once-round Telegraph craggy. Feeling ran so high among residents that two people were shot to death, one of them contractor George Gray, before the dynamiting was controlled.

Ignore for now the Greenwich Street steps that continue down the hill, often past a swarm of dragon flies, to Julius Castle. This is not the German castle, sometimes called "Layman's Folly," built in 1882. The original resort, where armored jousts were sometimes featured, burned in 1903.

Bear south instead to Filbert Street steps, past half-hidden houses and a skinny totem pole. Go down the concrete staircase and note the European flavor of the gardens, sculpture and imaginatively remodeled cottages. As you cross Montgomery Street, north of the Shadows restaurant, sniff the autumn air for the smell of high-wines. In 1906 wine saved Telegraph Hill from fire. Wine is still made sometimes on this hill, whose international past includes Chilean, Peruvian, Spanish, Italian, Irish and Swiss colonies.

Filbert steps become wooden near the postman's relay box lettered "Not for Deposit." Continue down to Darrell Place, which has the ingeniously-placed studio of sculptor Gert Murphy at number 60. The brilliant blue cottage is also hers.

The second offshoot downhill is Napier Lane, a wooden-sidewalk compound of sea-stained cottages which may be the oldest houses in San Francisco. For fifty years it has been a haven for cats, dogs and artists. Return to Filbert, noting the gardens created by Grace Marchant, long-time resident on the hill face. Comparable gardens on the Greenwich steps are tended by her daughter, Mrs. Desmond Heslett.

A penthouse, complete with lawn, is visible below the hill on a factory roof at Filbert and Sansome. Here the walker will be jolted by an abrupt transition from the tapestry of the hill to drab industry. The spartan can walk one block north and return via the Greenwich Street steps, reflecting, perhaps, how chance has created happily what the planners have yet to duplicate.

WASHINGTON SQUARE

Walking Time: Allow a morning to explore. Parking: None. Clothes: Inconspicuously urbane. Public Transportation: Buses 15, 30, 41, 39.

North Beach, a piece of verbal jetsam left by the tide that once lapped Chestnut between Stockton and Jones Streets, is synonymous in San Francisco with informality, hospitality and Little Italy. It is also a fairly well-defined city within the city, many of whose citizens remember the vineyards and olive trees in Tuscany, Sicily, Abruzzi, in Liguria, Apulia, Venezia and Lucca.

They brought the flavor with them. A stroll around North Beach is no substitute for a trip to the Mediterranean, but it offers a delicious antipasto. In North Beach, Broadway is the Rialto, Fisherman's Wharf the Porto, Aquatic Park the Lido, and Columbus Avenue the Via Romano. But it is to the piazza, Washington Square, that you must go to try the tempo of the community.

With a droll Venetian wink, Washington Square laughs at the advocates of single-use zoning. Its periphery can supply most sensible human needs. Its center, many more. Around its church, Sts. Peter and Paul, revolve the weddings, confirmations, saints' days, funerals and *festas* for feeding the soul. Two of them, the blessing of the fishing fleet in the name of the Blessed Lady del Lumé, on the first Sunday after October 1, and the Columbus Day parade and pageant, are among the most colorful festivals San Francisco celebrates.

Like the plaza in Sonoma, or any charming little continental city, the border of the square also has a post office, a theater, a pharmacy, a bakery that creates the St. Honoré cake, a good café, and other blandishments.

Benjamin Franklin upon a post office box is the curious piece of bric-a-brac in the heart of the square and a trio of firemen at work, the decoration on the northwest side. Perhaps no one has described the latter so well as poet Ron Loewinsohn, whose *The Mendacity of Sculpture* reads: ". . . one holding a Stricken Lady in his arms, another holding a nozzle/ a third with a horn, his right arm thrown up in a gesture, pointing: /Don't you see her! up there on the 4th floor,/ garlanded in flames! the child in her arms is screaming terrified/ —SHE'S GOING TO JUMP!

"That gesture for 23 years across Columbus Avenue, the bronze jacket / splattered with pigeonshit, out of whose sleeve a wrist & hand, also in bronze, / pointing / to a spot in the air 40 feet above the Palace Theater."

Benjamin Franklin is the gift of an unloved eccentric, Dr. Henry D. Cogswell. The volunteer firemen statue is the bequest of an equally eccentric, but much loved donor, Lillie Hitchcock Coit. The United States Coast and Geodetic Survey also left a trail marker, the tablet dated 1869–1880, which established the latitude and longitude of San Francisco.

It is the sweet and simple life of the square that gives it character, however. The old men reminiscing about sardine fishing, the zias and mamas gossiping while children play nearby, the shoppers who pause, the lovers who laugh, the diners who stroll, all share the informality.

Hospitality as a pattern was probably established long before the Italian community arrived. The genie of place who first occupied this site was a bountiful lady named Juana Briones y Miranda, whose adobe stood at Powell and Filbert Streets before 1843. The diary of a seafarer, William Thomes, of the crew of the *Admittance,* records that Juana Briones was generous with the milk, eggs and vegetables from her farm in North Beach. "If the men had some of the energy of that buxom, dark-faced lady," Thomes wrote, "California would have been a prosperous state, even before it was annexed to this country, and we would have had to fight harder than we did to get possession."

Walk uphill half a block on Stockton Street to see an early Bernard Maybeck building at number 1736. This was formerly the Telegraph Hill Neighborhood Association, founded by Alice Griffith, a pioneer San Francisco social worker. Here's one of the classical anecdotes about her: A sedentary type looked out of the window of the Pacific Union Club one day and saw Miss Griffith surrounded by a *group* of children of various ages and races. "Who was it that Miss Griffith married?" he asked the man in the next chair.

Uphill on Greenwich will take you quickly, via steps, to Coit Tower, sometimes past streetside conversational groups speaking animated Italian. The aria from an opera may come belting out of a bathroom window. Over all hovers a rich odor of garlic and oregano or basil, if you pass when dinner is cooking.

BROADWAY-BY-THE-HILL

Time: Allow an evening. **Distance:** Six blocks. **Clothes:** What you will. **Parking:** Prepare to pay. **Available Public Transportation:** Buses 41 or 15.

Broadway-by-the-Hill, the few short blocks from the tunnel to the bay, is San Francisco's neon ganglion, a nerve center for stimulating dissipation, and an extension of the old International Settlement where World War II troops had their last fling before shipping out to the Pacific. It is a gay way, a play way, a fey way; vulgar, mercenary; a mincing prince, a Pagliacci with tears in its beers, a W. C. Fields of a street, dressed to the nines, red-nosed, gluttonous and endlessly amusing.

For 77 years, Broadway was an earthy hip-swinging whore. Now this greedy ambisextrous witch, within the law since 1923 for San Francisco no longer has organized vice, gives itself airs like any other nouveau bourgeois. All come-on, bare asses and silicone under the twinkling sequins and red-velvet flocking, Broadway may dance with its belly bare and sigh romantically, but as ever, there are wise guttersnipe eyes under the mascara and a cash register where the soul should be.

Broadway's business, of course, is pleasure. This garish parish attracts not only the pleasure-seeker, and those unwary migratory birds known as tourists, a euphemism for "sucker," but all the night-people who tend the trap lines—the sleans, gleets, flits, fags, crooks, bookies, "semiprofessional" hustlers and other night-blooming cacti. But for all that, Broadway is to stroll. The glittery-jittery human comedy makes this street a delightful nightly promenade.

To check the action, begin this walk after 9 P.M. at Clark's Point, as the corner of Battery and Broadway was once named. The early notable settler, William S. Clark, first of the lawless speculators, gave San Francisco a baptism in land-greed. Clark arrived from Maryland in 1846, discovered he could purchase only one lot in his own name and promptly employed people to buy lots and deed them to him. He also built the first wharf in San Francisco at which ships could moor. By 1886 he could have written "How to Make Millions in Real Estate." Over Battery Street, which took its name from Captain John B. Montgomery's gun emplacements, a freeway now threatens, hovering like a great governmental blue pencil of the future, ready to delete Broadway, despite all its history and merriment, in one devastating stroke.

Clark had some interesting neighbors: his wharf was the approach to the Barbary Coast, and Osborne Street, for example, was the site of three early hotels. It is not unlikely that at least one of them made a good business shanghaiing sailors. It also led to "Little Chile," once noted for its prostitutes, some of whom performed with animals at the Fierce Grizzly and the Boar's Head public houses. "Honest" Harry Meiggs, an early municipal bilker; the "Sydney ducks"; the Hounds and the Regulators, blackguards disbanded from Stevenson's regiment, have all been denizens of Broadway. In almost any Broadway restaurant, bar, club or coffee-house—Enrico's, the Matador, Vanessi's, Casa Madrid, to name but four—the walker pausing for refreshment can speculate on the rip-roaring sins that have been perpetrated in lustier, more primitive times, exactly where he is sitting. More than one man swung for it on Broadway, too, for the Broadway gallows and jail once stood at Romulo Street. Broadway has always been a swinging street.

Today, although the pleasure-bent usually do not notice, there are also two schools, a bookstore, a sausage factory, clothing shops, groceries, galleries, a housing project and a church, the Mexican Nuestra Señora de Guadalupe. Before dawn on December 12, the Mexican population serenades the Virgin in this church, which sits on the foundations of the first synagogue of San Francisco. No other street in the city teems so constantly, sleeps so little and works so hard, despite the tyranny of motor traffic that has been thrust upon it, as Broadway, where North Beach meets Chinatown.

RUSSIAN HILL

1 MACONDRAY LANE   5 FISHERMAN'S WHARF

2 RUSSIAN HILL PLACE   6 AQUATIC PARK

3 THE WIGGLY STREET   7 MARITIME MUSEUM

4 GHIRARDELLI SQUARE   8 THE CANNERY

9 FORT MASON

MARINA BLVD.
MacDOWELL AVE.
GARDENS
MARKER
MUNICIPAL PIER
VICTORIAN PARK
TONQUIN
FISHERMAN'S WHARF 5
BLACK POINT
7 MARITIME MUSEUM
AQUATIC PARK
6
8
JEFFERSON
THE CANNERY
BEACH
4
NORTH POINT
9 FORT MASON
BAY
MacARTHUR
FRANCISCO
FRANKLIN
OFFICERS' CLUB
VAN NESS
POLK
COLUMBUS
GHIRARDELLI SQUARE
CHESTNUT
RUSSIAN HILL PLACE 2
MACONDRAY LANE 1
3 LOMBARD
COOLBRITH PARK
GREENWICH
LARKIN
FILBERT
UNION
GREEN
ALTA VISTA
FALLON
VALLEJO
FLORENCE
BROADWAY
HYDE
LEAVENWORTH
JONES
TAYLOR
MASON
POWELL

RUSSIAN HILL

Walking Time: 30 minutes. **Distance:** Five steep blocks. **Clothes:** Urbane. **Transportation:** Hyde Street cable car, No. 30 bus.

For the confirmed city dweller who loves San Francisco for her inspired and civilized livability Heaven is a place called Russian Hill.

To understand why, you must get out on foot and embrace it with all five senses. There are a hundred good places to start, but the apex of the "wiggly-block" on Lombard at Hyde Street is as rewarding as any. Look north. There is the famous sweeping picture of the bay as painted by Dong Kingman and dozens of lesser-known artists, photographed as a hallmark of the city for travel posters, fashion ads and television programs, and immortalized in verse by Gelett Burgess in "The Ballad of the Hyde Street Grip." It beckons you to walk in this direction. If you do, you will walk in glory all the way and find the pleasures of Aquatic Park and the treasures of the Maritime Museum when you reach the shore below.

Resist this Lorelei and shut your eyes instead. Sniff! If the wind is right, the fresh salt-sea tang that comes in on the tide will mingle with flower scent from an old garden nearby. Listen! The cables clunk underfoot, a gripman plays a happy dingdong song as he nears the Bay Street crossing, often to the counterpoint of a distant low-growling diaphone.

Look west. The enticing George Sterling park on the right also beckons, and its charms include tennis courts, paths to stroll, a sandbox where toddlers play, a mall where old people reminisce in the sun, a suntrap where bikinis bloom, a memorial bench to poet George Sterling, who lived at the corner of Hyde and Greenwich, and best of all, space and green trees, to give perspective to the luxurious apartment towers whose shared front yard it seems to be.

Resist the park too. South is a congenial shopping confluence where superb ice cream, fresh oysters, caviar and Belgian endive are among the staples. Near it are culs-de-sac, little lanes, parklets and all the ranges of housing, from huddles of hovels to peerless penthouses, the city has to offer.

Look east. In the distance Coit Tower looms virilely out of its copse on Telegraph Hill, with North Beach snug below. Downtown, Chinatown, Jackson Square, Union Square are all in easy walking distance. Just underfoot are the recurves of Lombard Street, zigging and zagging through the hydrangea bushes Peter Bercut inspired his neighbors to plant.

Follow this mellow-bricked road. Halfway down the stair is a wider stair known as Montclair Terrace, where 65, designed by Gardner Dailey, and 66, by Henry Hill, will interest architectural fans. Bear left on Leavenworth, then right on Chestnut. These blocks are part of a section selected by Margaret von Barnevelt Cole for a study called "The Urban Aesthetic" because of its superb urban delights. Feast the eye on the brown Willis Polk house, the pink Bakewell house, the gray home of the Berigans, each set in greenery and sloping on the cliff. Across the street ringed with fine trees in cobblestone setts is the San Francisco Art Institute. North on Jones Street will bring you past the garden of the school, which has a treehouse and sculpture-in-progress visible as you walk.

Before you leave the hill, look back. Walt Whitman, the great urban poet, might have been singing of it in his *Leaves of Grass,* when he wrote: "The place where the great city stands is not . . . the place of the tallest and costliest buildings . . . nor the place of the most numerous population [although Russian Hill has both]. Where the city stands with the brawniest breed of orators and bards /Where the city stands that is beloved by these, and loves them in return, and understands them . . . There the great city stands . . ."

RUSSIAN HILL PLACE

Walking Time: 20 minutes. **Distance:** 5 city blocks. **Parking:** None. **Public Transportation:** Hyde Street cable car to Vallejo Street. Return from Vallejo via Powell and Mason cable car on Mason.

Upper Bohemia is a worldwide microcosm bounded by Parnassus, Nirvana, Limbo and Infinity. Its places of legend are equally widespread, and in San Francisco, Pop Demarest's compound, a serene green cranny on the eastern apex of the Russian Hill dogleg, ranks among the favorites. Like the Italian beach where Trelawney snatched the burning heart of Shelley from the pyre, like the public square in Boston where Mencken sold his banned book despite the Watch and Ward Society, like the second-best bed mentioned in Shakespeare's will, or in our time like Costello's Third Avenue pub in New York where Tim would cash a check for a writer after banking hours, if he admired his literary style, there is a reason for the legend of the place. Legends always have the same reason—a better-than-human dimension.

In his compound of small cottages, where rents were within reach of such struggling writers as Ambrose Bierce, Will and Wallace Irwin, Gelett Burgess, Ina Coolbrith, Charlie Dobie and Frank Norris, Pop Demarest created the better human dimension himself. He wrought it out of the direct application of the Golden Rule to the art of living, but it would have embarrassed him if anyone said so. It was a tough climb to the compound, perched between the Broadway and Vallejo Street steps above Taylor, on what is now Florence, but the living was civilized and Pop didn't come up like thunder the split second the rent was due.

Pop went on a binge each month and danced by the light of the moon. He was also reputed to be a music-loving hermit and to own eighteen cats. Helga Iversen Wall, of 894 Chestnut Street, says "I knew old Pop rather well, since he lived in his hovel right underneath the cottage I formerly occupied. I can attest to the cats, to the recordings and to the caves under the hill. I was still living in the compound when old Pop did himself in by falling one night in a slight stupor of drink and breaking some bones. He was finally taken to the hospital, and rumor had it that he couldn't stand the cleanliness of it!"

Pop first took refuge in a cistern on the compound two weeks after the fire of '06. Thereafter he kept it stocked as a sort of helter-skelter shelter. After his death in 1939, friends found in his apartment several thousand gramophone records, a mound of chickenbones and sardine cans, and a twenty-year collection of cobwebs, some adorned with papier-mâché spiders. No one counted the cats.

That's the legend. What it doesn't say is that between 1872 and 1939 five generations of San Francisco writers found the compound compatible with their human needs. To find the place walk to the juncture of Vallejo and Jones. Two very narrow ramps and a staircase within an abutment lead up to the 1000 block of

Vallejo. At the top is a constricted trefoil of short culs-de-sac. Russian Hill Place goes to the north. On it are two Ward-designed houses, numbers 2 and 4. Willis Polk designed 1013–15–17–19 Vallejo. Florence Place is the street on the south. Behind the oak trees on the right is the home of Putnam Livermore, well-known conservationist and descendant of a California pioneer. It was his mother who planted the trees. On the other side of the street are two houses built in 1895 by Marshall, 1032 and 1034, all charming behind their garden gates. Two others have been torn down to be replaced by apartments. Within a three block radius, two other high-rising cell-blocks are also destroying neighborhood continuity as San Francisco converts from livability to what James Bone has called New York, "a city of dreadful height."

Willis Polk himself lived in the cottage on the southeast corner on the steps at 1013 Vallejo. Cottages like Pop's can be glimpsed through beautiful plantings as one walks downhill toward Ina Coolbrith Park, an oasis in memory of the much-loved librarian and poetess who once lived near. Her home was a salon for writers for many years. Across Taylor Street, a path leads into the park. Another set of steps will take the walker downhill past Alta Vista Terrace, a compound much like Pop Demarest's. Look for it on the north side of the street behind an iron gate.

MACONDRAY LANE

Walking Time: Twenty minutes at most. **Distance:** Two city blocks. **Nearby Public Transportation:** Union Street Bus 41. **Clothing:** Casual. **Available Parking:** Very little.

Like Catfish Row, or Germelshausen or Gloccamorra, Macondray Lane is a dream. It is also one of the secret walks of San Francisco, a well-shared secret of a knowledgeable few, and the home of a privileged handful of people who eat their cake of urbanity and have rural seclusion too.

Every imaginative American has seen Macondray Lane in what William Butler Yeats called the Land of Heart's Desire. It is a canvas by Rockwell Kent, out of Old Lyme, Connecticut, by way of Hollywood. Vines tumble over an archway that leads one past old trees and unusual cottages to a special cottage where beauty has no ebb. Time sings an endless song in a familiar, full-bodied voice (Bing Crosby's to anyone older than thirty). The tune is "Take me where the daisies cover the country lanes . . ."

The wonder is that Macondray Lane, a footpath, hides, not in Orinda, but on Russian Hill in a congested part of the city surrounded, at a modest estimate, by 5,000 people in a half-mile radius. It is a deceptive anachronism, a two-block-long accident of place in time, and its enchantment is reserved for the walker.

The ideal time to take this walk is a weekday morning in the dry season. The highest entrance to the lane begins at Leavenworth between Green and Union Streets. It seems at first inspection to be a vestigial alley serving some apartment buildings. Unexpectedly soon it turns into a narrow, wooden walk, railed to prevent the pedestrian from falling down a steep embankment. Pass the modest house that fronts on the lane and go up close to the railing. Suddenly you have the illusion that you are in a treehouse, for two great gnarled albizzia trees, whose trunks are far below, shelter you.

Beneath their branches is a scene out of Booth Tarkington or Sinclair Lewis—a broad lawn, two yellow clapboard houses, vintage 1907, a vegetable garden, a rabbit hutch and a studio.

When you can tear yourself away, follow the path along the buildings that tower above. Flowers grow in crannies at shoulder height. A song sparrow may warble. The shrubs through which the path leads give a tantalizing peek-a-boo of the beautiful blue bay and the gardens below.

At Jones Street, the entrance to the lane looks like a garden gate. This illusion of privacy, together with the solid ledge of rock it hugs, and one or two experiences with land slippage above, may account for Macondray's resistance to that dubious force we sometimes mislabel Progress.

Once within the vine-heavy arch, Macondray Lane assumes some of the character embodied in Japanese gardens. Stepping stones change from brick to cobble to random concrete. The way bends and twists. Sculptural trees, cats and garbage cans share the drowsy sunlight. A line of cottages, no two alike, but all built to the manageable human scale of vision, fronts on this path.

The casual walker may meet a resident, gardening in front of her cottage, who when pressed will tell one that the lane, now named for a pioneer merchant, F. W. Macondray, was once called Lincoln

Alley. Or Mr. John Tampcke, of number 56, who would rather talk about the colorful, bohemian life of the lane. "The old Macondray Street Theater was located in the basement of my house," he says; "and number 17 was the home of the artist Cadenasso."

Number 17, a green and white Victorian, is almost at the end of the lane. Two great old jade trees flank it. Inexplicably, for a long time an inverted bathtub stood alongside the house, cast iron feet in the air, as anachronistic as Macondray Lane itself.

Poets have long loved the lane and among those one might have met on it in earlier years were Ina Coolbrith and Charles and Eleanore Ross, all vital figures in San Francisco's literary life.

Once down the steps to Taylor Street, the mood of enchantment breaks. If you think you made it up in a reverie, go walk it again.

FISHERMAN'S WHARF

Walking Time: Half a day at least. **Distance:** What you will. **Nearby Public Transportation:** Bus 19 to Jefferson and Leavenworth. **Available Parking:** Dreary, especially weekends and Fridays. **Clothing:** Warm and casual.

Facility 49. This is not a comfort station. It is what Government, which has a knack for grouping things into dry lifelessness, calls that busy and exciting section of San Francisco shorefront which lies between Taylor and Hyde Streets. The rest of us, and especially the Chamber of Commerce, call the periphery of it Fisherman's Wharf.

The truth is rather more, for there is a Fisherman's Wharf the tourists do not know. The area shelters a double community, a swan-swoose, and the only way to find it is to shuck off those hard-top insulating shells called cars and get out on foot.

We all fancy we know the swoose of sea-food restaurants, excursion and party boats, gimcracker-crumby souvenirs and pitchmen honking and tonking. There are those who think it is the swan.

It's a rare bird, all right, but not nearly so beguiling as the one hidden in plain sight, like Poe's purloined letter. You will find it on the piers known as the Finger Wharf, north of Jefferson Street between Leavenworth and Hyde. It is a workaday world, charming in its simplicity and good humor, of fishermen, shipwrights, chandlers, netmakers, divers, crabpickers and packers. It cannot be captured by pointing a camera at Nick Rescino, owner of the *Lovely Martha,* and saying "Smile, Captain!"

You must walk on the piers, forget your watch, and linger sometimes by a cleat along the dockside. You must look with your heart and understand, as a jet goes by overhead, that the harvest of the seas is still pulled in by men in small boats, frequently at their own peril.

Not that they seem concerned about it along the Finger Wharf. To see for yourself, turn in by the sign which says "Chrysler Radio Telephones Depth Indicators." Within thirty paces you are away from the tourist's world.

There in front of the Crab Boat Owners' Association on a bench in the sun sit the old men who fished long ago. They are welcome here. When the rains come, they are welcome inside too, to play Trisetta—three sevens—or Biscola. They can see the ways where boats are in for repair. They can watch the small boats pass. And the fishermen . . . Banjo, Coochie, Diesel Sam, Freckles, Bandito . . . most of whom stop and talk, sometimes in Italian, and to read the chalkboard nailed on the building.

Walk on past the Wharfingers, past the Boicelli and Boss Machine Works, to the palm of the Finger Wharf. Except for a restaurant intrusion from the more commercial world this is still the genuine place.

This is just a taste of what there is to see in the walking working world behind the apron of Fisherman's Wharf. "Long Minico," the netmaker, Caldun and Tracey, the divers, the Gateway Shipwright, Frank's Pompeii, the Fish and Game boat *Nautilus,* Hogan's, the skyblue portable public privies, the hoists, the dragboats, are all there to discover.

The swan labeled Facility 49 is not to be found in one day. You must return from time to time in a credulous mood. Who knows, Ducky, if you really seek the swan, you may even stumble upon Lady Tyles, a glamorous, Australian demimyth, or learn why sixty-six pounds of Babbit-bearing is not to be sneezed at as salvage.

THE NORTHERN WATERFRONT

Walking Time: Give it half a day and stay for lunch or dinner. **Distance:** The circumnavigation of 2½ acres on many levels. **Parking:** In the garage down under. **Public Transportation:** Polk Street bus 19. Stockton bus 30. Embarcadero bus 32. Hyde Street cable car.

Ghirardelli Square. Say these musical syllables happily if you love San Francisco. Let your voice hold overtones of commingled awe, reverence and gratitude. Say it with the lilt of delight, eyes shining, that a child acclaims on Christmas morning the one toy, the special toy, the meaningful toy of his dreams.

This is what Ghirardelli Square really is: A gift to the City of San Francisco by a visionary, and now legendary man, William Matson Roth.

Ours is a time when most developers, given 2½ acres of waterfront or hillside, stash any pretense to civic conscience in the deep freeze. Some do it even while flaunting memberships in groups devoted to civic betterment. While dollar signs dance in their minds, they pirate for all time the value of any adjacent land behind them with towers or blockbusters that would make Babel blush. Not so the civilized Mr. Roth. As Scott Newhall, a knowledgeable editor, wrote of him, "Bill Roth has put his money where his mouth is." Quietly and gently, at no small sacrifice to himself, Mr. Roth created, with the help of architects Wurster, Bernardi and Emmons, a new use for an old complex of factory buildings, which put the amenities of city living before the percentage of dollar return on his investment.

His generosity has been contagious. Good taste, as it happens, can be profitable. Encouraged by the smashing success of Ghirardelli Square, just a block and a half away, Leonard Martin has tried to top it with an enclave that is equally exciting, The Cannery, whose architect was Joe Esherick. Fromm and Sichel have followed the lead with a wine museum, designed by Worley Wong, so entrancing it calls for a pilgrimage from anyone who can lift a snifter.

For the walker this highmindedness boils down to a very pleasant outing. The Northern Waterfront, where these and dozens of other places worth discovering are located, is a great place to go. A place that is fun to see and where it is fun to be. At every ramp, turn, stair, balcony, ledge and level, the heart leaps up refreshed by the splendor of the bay. Folksingers, pipers, mimes, dancers, puppeteers, and guitarists may be performing in any court. Twilight brings sweet tristesse. Linger by the Ruth Asawa Fountain in Ghirardelli's east plaza at sundown and you may find yourself unconsciously humming "Harbor Lights."

To see for yourself, pick up a Hyde Street cable car downtown at Powell and Market Streets and ride almost to the end of the line. As you swoop down the Hyde Street hill, the red brick and cream clock-tower building, signature of Ghirardelli Square, becomes visible over the rooftops. With this as a landmark, get off on North Point Street and walk one block west to Larkin Street. Under the clock, step into Design Research to see the Ghirardelli eagle trademark set in the tiles just as architect William Mooser II designed it in 1893 for the Ghirardelli Chocolate Company. Until 1963, the tantalizing smell of chocolate wafted uphill from the factory. Meander through the store to come out into the east plaza whose Casbah quality is immediately apparent. There are free guide maps at the information kiosk and you'll need one. If you can resist Susanne Lemmon's Ghirardelli Bookstore, and Senor Pico, walk west to find another plaza where the Mandarin, J. D. Browne, and Edelweiss are instant eyecatchers. Nearby are shops for any whim. I especially like the Great Eastern Trading Company, Richter's unique music box boutique, Come Fly a Kite, whose proprietor often gives noontime kiteflying lessons, and To Put It In, which has pots, among other containers.

Before you've spent every cent, locate the Maritime Museum, across from the lower perimeter of the square. Then, after a visit, head away from it, east, past the Buena Vista Cafe to find the Wine Museum of San Francisco. The Cannery is half a block further.

At The Cannery, The Black Sheep, a needlework center, can't keep in stock the witty Oriental hanging whose calligraphy says something infamous about what will fall on you if you sit under the tree in which the bird of happiness perches. The Chelsea Shop is known for its French porcelain condomiers, Amerind for its Alaskan and Indian crafts, The African for some things from a warmer clime.

Gluttons should not miss the Ben Jonson, as in O Rare, an English pub. Its restaurant has a museum piece, the Long Hall of St. Albyns, designed and built in 1609 by Inigo Jones. Wenches serve viands before a crackling fire. There is also a gourmet market in The Cannery, where the choicest fresh caviar is flown in daily.

If that special artifact from Samarkand or India still eludes you, walk east on North Point Street to find, beyond Fisherman's Wharf at Taylor Street, the labyrinthine rabbit's warren that is Cost Plus. When import duty keeps world travelers from lugging back treasures from any of 40-odd countries, they often find them here cheaper than abroad. Christmas, all over again.

AQUATIC PARK

Walking Time: At least an hour. **Distance:** Approximately 1½ miles. **Nearby Public Transportation:** Hyde Street cable car, bus 19 on Polk Street, bus 47 on Van Ness. **Available Parking:** At this writing, excellent. **Clothing:** Casual. Take a sweater.

What the silver Seine is to Paris, Aquatic Park, 34½ acres of shore nestled at the foot of Russian Hill, is to San Francisco. Here the human comedy is played in slow motion with a yawn in a stage setting splendid enough for Pericles. To walk around it is a rare, cosmopolitan adventure.

On the promenade along the beach, one may sometimes observe an ocelot, paraded on a gold leash by an elegant young lady. A kangaroo, an osprey, a dying shark, a trio of skin divers, a machete-twirling sword dancer, a bagpiper, or a juggler practicing on the sand may be all in a day's walk round Aquatic.

On any fair day, the walker will surely see small children, wet retrievers, gulls, Olympic swimmers, virile bocce ball players, less virile beach boys, fishermen in assorted sizes and colors, sanitary engineers testing the water for E. coli, pensioners sitting out of the wind and bikini-clad sun worshipers.

The cable car turntable at Beach and Hyde Streets is a likely place to start this walk. Noon on a sunny day is the best of times.

Since the terrain is fairly flat, well paved and set about with benches, walkers only recently liberated from their wheels, old people and new mothers may safely essay it.

The walker will inevitably feel his eyes drawn first to the beauty of the bay, clasped loverlike here in the curving arm of Municipal Pier. Turn any way next and there is something of interest to see. The stately grove of trees west of the pier was called Point Medanos by the earliest Spanish settlers. It was here in 1797 that Governor Diego de Borica had a battery named San Jose built by his engineer, Alberto de Cordoba, "to impede the anchorage of any hostile vessel in La Yerba Buena."

Battery San Jose didn't impede a hostile vessel called the *Portsmouth*. By the 1850's, when General and Mrs. John C. Frémont moved into the property, it was called Black Point and the six eight-pound cannons of the battery disappeared. It's odd to think of the General as a squatter, but his heirs are still crying "foulplay" in the courts. Fort Mason squats on the point, now part of the Golden Gate National Recreation Area.

At one end of the sandy beach is a complex of white buildings, housing three venerable rowing clubs. Across Hyde Street is the old Haslett Warehouse Number One, destiny unwritten. Across Beach Street is the Buena Vista, a pub that is a contender for the glory of having invented Irish Coffee, and filled at this time of day with lunching businessmen.

A colorful spot in the periphery of the Park is a cluster of barn-red buildings in a green lawn which looks for all the world like a colored engraving by Edward Bosqui, Esq. The canted old red brick building was occupied by the pioneer Columbia Woolen Mill when banker William C. Ralston swam to his death in 1875. From 1897 until 1964 the enticing odor of Ghirardelli's Chocolate, organized in the 1850's and once situated in Old Town, pervaded the air of Black Point from this spot.

The smells used to be riper. Canneries, smelters, stables, slaughterhouses and carriage works once stood near. In contradistinction to the common trend, over the years industry has been displaced here by residences, mostly modest. The yellow Kodak building is an eye-catching exception.

The dominant eye-catcher in Aquatic Park belongs to the people. This is the Casino, a great stranded concrete battleship, which houses the San Francisco Senior Center, public dressing rooms, sandwich counter and the Maritime Museum. Salt water buffs will undoubtedly defect here to see the soul-stirring, sea-going artifacts of clipper days.

The joy of discovering the unparalleled view from the end of Municipal Pier, the fog horns, the tunnel, the railroad tracks whose ties can be walked, the almost legible headstones in the water near the Sea Scout Base, the bocce ball courts, Hyde Street Wharf, and many more charming surprises await the intrepid explorer on foot.

How long Aquatic will continue to glisten in the sun is anybody's guess. Two ominous shadows are already threatening to darken your sand and mine, for whoever saw bridge or freeway that cast no palls at all.

MARITIME MUSEUM

Walking Time: Allow an hour. **Clothes:** Rubber-soled shoes. **Parking:** Only fair. **Public Transportation:** Bus 19 takes you to the door.

The call of the running tide, "the wild call, the clear call, that may not be denied," hits many San Franciscans whenever there's a salty onshore breeze.

When it does, those who have boats go sailing on the bay. Those who have time and money take a cruise. The rest of us "hoist up the John B. sails and see how the mainsail sets" at the San Francisco Maritime Museum. The vicarious sailing in the concrete ship at the foot of Polk Street is one of the choice walks in the city.

The location of the Maritime Museum within the Aquatic Park Casino is a marriage made in heaven. It is difficult to believe the building was not created for the purpose, yet Architect William Mooser III designed it in 1935, long before the museum was a mote in Director Karl Kortum's long glass. A restaurant and later a USO center dallied in the Casino, but these were shipboard romances.

It is rare to see the work of three generations of architects from one family in one glance, yet this was possible from the doorstep of the casino until just recently. William Mooser II designed many of the Ghirardelli buildings. His father created the handsome old Fontana warehouse, now razed.

Before entering, look west toward the colorful new canopy on the bocce ball court. A tall ivy-covered brick chimney of the San Francisco Waterworks, favorite landmark of old sea captains, stood there until the thirties. Face east to see an emerging mecca beckoning transportation buffs. A bright pavilion at the Hyde Street cable car turnaround, part of the Victorian, gas-lighted plaza, has emerged recently. Haslett warehouse, well-served by spur tracks of the Belt Line railroad, could house historical steam locomotives, cable cars, stages, Conestoga wagons and such.

Gallant old craft that might have mouldered to ghostliness on some forgotten Rotten Row are anchored at the foot of Hyde Street for the public to visit. They have names that would excite a folk-laureate, the ferry boat *Eureka,* the lumber schooner *C. A. Thayer,* the steam schooner *Wapama,* the scow-schooner *Alma.* Like the better-known *Balclutha,* the beautiful full-rigger which rounded Cape Horn seventeen times under sail, they are part of the Maritime Museum. There is a modest fee to go aboard them.

A red buoy just inside the door of the Maritime Museum welcomes contributions, but there is no fee. Once aboard the lugger and the whirl is fine. The great anchor of the *Constitution* vies with figureheads of Lord Clive, who once adorned the *Himalaya,* and Mary, Queen of Scots, from the bow of the *Star of Scotland,* and other salty artifacts. Great ship models stand proudly under sail as they once stood out through the Golden Gate. Downeasters, deep-watermen, clippers, bumboats, barges and tugs are all captured here in legend, record and photograph, bringing to life the stuff dreams of seaborne derring-do are made on. Upstairs the saga of the seas swells with romance. It reaches a factual crest in the little oval pilot room on the third floor where an excellent research staff for serious marine historians is located in the museum office.

On the starboard side of the casino is a locker room. (To find it go around the Senior Center until you parallel the beach, whose white sand, incidentally, was imported from Monterey.) Worth seeing is the eight-oared shell overhead in which Coach Ky Ebright's University of California team brought home an Olympic championship in 1928.

If Able and Baker mean Cain's brother and Blum's to you, watch which doors you walk through. An old salt occasionally tells visitors that the ship's flags painted on the lintels spell out an old sea chantey whose refrain goes "Blow ye winds of morning, oh, blow ye winds heigh-ho."

He's taking poetic liberties. The flags are nothing but the locker-room signs, rigged out in a disguise.

FORT MASON

Walking Time: A brisk twenty minutes or a leisurely hour. **Distance:** Roughly a mile. **Parking:** Only fair. **Available Public Transportation:** Stockton bus 30 or Potrero bus 47 to Bay and Van Ness. **Clothing:** Tweedy walking clothes and stout shoes. High heels will not do.

The secret, scenic walk that walkers share with one another, as gourmets share a vintage wine, is to be found on Fort Mason. It is a cliffside ramble through the trees above the bay, redolent of a million sad, war-torn farewells, fewer glad returns, and all the tunes of glory. It is not a secret that is confided lightly.

But if you are a true lover of San Francisco, if you know in your heart the greatest legacies we could leave our city are the priceless, irreplaceable bits of breathing space that make her special, come with me to the corner of Van Ness and Bay Streets. Come at 5 P.M. when the single boom of the sunset gun, by proximity, once made peace seem ever dearer.

Walk north through the wrought-iron pedestrian gate along a curving lane toward the building marked as the Fort Mason Officers' Mess. The community of homes you pass was a parking lot in World War II. The silent melody in the air is "Sentimental Journey" as played by Glenn Miller.

It makes a quick *segue* to "Tenting Tonight on the Old Camp Ground" as you reach the Officers' Club which is fronted by a carriage turnaround, dating, like the building, to 1855. Historians identify this building as Brook House Number One, but it is McDowell Hall to the men of the post. For many years it housed the commanding generals of Fort Mason. McDowell, Sheridan, Ord and Arthur McArthur are among the old soldiers who have not died but only faded away from this spot.

The old administration building now houses the headquarters of the Golden Gate National Recreation Area. Ramshackle temporary buildings west of it have come down to accommodate new recreation grounds.

Veer west to Franklin Street where at least one walker has been surprised to hear issuing from the post chapel carillon what he thought was a lively version of "How Dry I Am." Tune detectives could have told him it was the old gospel hymn "Oh, Happy Day."

General George Marshall was the kindly man who approved the chapel's unusual Spanish tower. He did it as a favor to Maj. Gen. Frederick Gilbreth, who could not stand GI church architecture.

Bearing north on Franklin to the tune of "The Girl I Left Behind Me," the walker will pass through the original cantonment created on orders of President Millard Fillmore issued November 6, 1850, to Col. Richard Mason, military governor of California. To history buffs, this is hallowed ground. Brook House Number Two (split off from One long ago); Haskell House, where Senator David Broderick died in 1859 after his duel with the terrible-tempered Justice Terry; and Palmer House, are the last three on the right. The five small houses across the street, and two more around the corner on Funston Road, date from 1863.

Jog to the right beyond Palmer House following the sidewalk to a tree-sheltered lawn accessible only on foot. As private as it seems, the public is welcome here (until nightfall). The historical marker which announces "Bateria San José" tells the story. "In 1797," it says, "the Spanish constructed on this site a gun battery . . . for the protection of La Yerba Buena Anchorage. The anchorage was approximately a quarter of a mile to the east from this point and is now known as Aquatic Park."

Pathfinder John Frémont, sometime squatter, spiked the guns of this battery, and built his home west of the site. It is no longer standing. The cliffside paths he strolled are paved and provided with benches at the best view vantages. The lower walk skirts Black Point Pumping House and meanders through trees given by John McLaren. The higher walk goes through the commanding general's garden behind Haskell House. Both join below the Officers' Club lawn and bring the walker out alongside tennis courts adjoining the club. To end this walk requires an imaginary medley that spans a century and a half. Try, for sighs, plantation voices in "The Year of Jubilow" followed by "The Yellow Rose of Texas" on shrill fifes, blending into George M. Cohan singing "Hello Central, Give Me No Man's Land." The finale could be an astral chorus led by the Andrews Sisters beginning "There's a Troopship A-Leavin' Bombay." Maybe you remember it as "Bless 'Em All."

COW HOLLOW

1 UNION STREET

2 PALACE OF FINE ARTS

3 MARINA GREEN

4 GOLDEN GATE PROMENADE (EAST END)

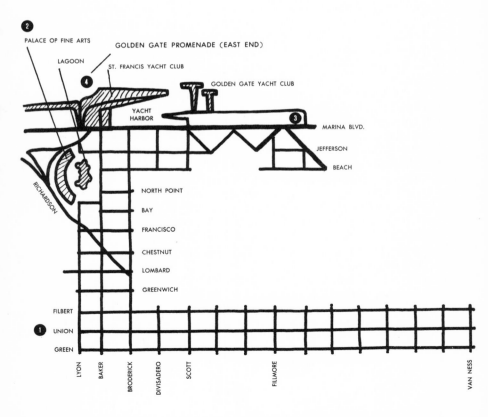

2
PALACE OP FINE ARTS

GOLDEN GATE PROMENADE (EAST END)

LAGOON

ST. FRANCIS YACHT CLUB

4

GOLDEN GATE YACHT CLUB

YACHT
HARBOR

3

MARINA BLVD.

JEFFERSON

BEACH

RICHARDSON

NORTH POINT

BAY

FRANCISCO

CHESTNUT

LOMBARD

GREENWICH

FILBERT

1 UNION

GREEN

LYON BAKER BRODERICK DIVISADERO SCOTT FILLMORE VAN NESS

UNION STREET

Walking Time: Allow a morning if you like to browse. **Distance:** Fourteen city blocks. **Clothes:** Citified but casual. **Available Public Transportation:** Buses 41, 45.

One of the joys of the city is that you can walk around a corner and find a different world. Cow Hollow, once an idyllic retreat of market gardens, pretty dairymaids, dunes, springs and orchards, is such a world.

You will not find Cow Hollow on the map, but Union Street between Van Ness and Lyon is the heart of it. The walker who brings perceptive eyes can still find the droll, bucolic neighborhood of folklore clinging to Union, as incongruous as telltale wisps of straw on a Hattie Carnegie gown.

Union is a woman's street with flowers in her hair, fripperies in her boutiques, and a fancy selection of goods for conspicuous consumption, among them crab Mornay, pre-Columbian fetishes, an unfading potpourri and Tarot cards in her shops. As the leer-while-you-steer car-poolers from Marin have discovered, it also has the prettiest girls and young matrons, shopping or waiting for the buses.

The shops that serve them are housed in old Victorians, former hotel dining rooms, stables, and in a few places, buildings built for the purposes they now serve. It is a colorful street and on it the walker may meet white-gloved, but hatless Junior Leaguers, younger buds in shorts, business girls, grand dames, or an old lady who pushes four dogs in a perambulator.

The place to begin this walk of rediscovery is Van Ness and Union. The best time, a weekday morning. There is no trace today of Laguna Pequena, or Washerwoman's Lagoon, which once lay between Franklin, Octavia, Filbert and Lombard and gave its name to Laguna Street, but a block past Sherman School (named for the general who marched through Georgia) the walker will find an oasis of green.

This old-fashioned garden within a picket fence is the first tangible vestige of the Cow Hollow of yesterday. Beside it stands one of San Francisco's two remaining octagonal houses, home of the National Society of Colonial Dames. It was built in 1857, once stood across the street, and is open to the public for 50 cents, the second and fourth Thursday afternoons each month.

Just uphill Allyne Park stand on the site of the former Victorian home of the octogenarian sisters, Edith and Lucy Allyne, who never lived anywhere else. Granddaughters of pioneer Ephraim W. Burr, onetime mayor of San Francisco, the sisters inherited a $3 million fortune and the house, built in 1871, from their father. Part of its fittings included an Oriental porcelain urn once used as a watering trough for Captain Allyne's cow.

Not this cow, but hundreds of others and the dairies which served the city, gave Cow Hollow its name. Charlton Place, a cul-de-sac which juts off Union, is reputed to have been a milk-wagon loading yard for one of these.

Other vestigial landmarks along the street are the Dresden blue Victorian, and number 2056, which has contemporary wrought-iron sculpture posing on its lawn under an old palm.

Worth a look too are the Metro Theater, home of San Francisco's International Film Festival, the Mingei-Ya, a Japanese country-style restaurant, the pot-garden at 2147, the waterfall in the window of the Rio Theater, the Artist's Co-Op, The Deli, Perry's, and Kelly Brothers' grocery, which hasn't changed in 40 years.

The street changes pace beyond Steiner. Elegant houses, at least one of them a hundred years old, lie beyond the Episcopal Church known jocularly to its parishioners as "St. Mary's Diversion." A gift of pioneer editor Frank Pixley, the land of St. Mary's holds the last easily accessible trace of Cow Hollow. Go through the lych-gate, which looks as though it should stand on an English hillside. There in a tiled fountain, a spring early dairy farmers hoped would give water till the cows came home, bubbles on, long after the last cow of Cow Hollow is gone.

PALACE OF FINE ARTS

Walking Time: A brisk twenty minutes. Distance: Approximately eight city blocks. Nearby Public Transportation: Bus 30 to Bay and Broderick. Parking: Good. Clothes: Walking tweeds.

Sweet are the uses of property, but seldom simple. An exception is the Costanoan Indian shell-mound once known as Strawberry Island. In the 180-odd years which pass for forever in San Francisco, its use has been singularly uncomplicated. It was conceived as a place of recreation and residence by its first and only non-governmental owners, pioneer Rudolph Herman and his family, who received it as a state land grant in the· 1850's. They beautified it and called it Harbor View Park.

Recreational and residential it remains to this day, incorporated into the state park grounds of the Palace of Fine Arts, romantic relic of the Panama Pacific International Exposition of 1915, which celebrated the completion of that busy ditch, the Panama Canal. One San Franciscan, Mrs. William Woods Adams, a granddaughter of Rudolph Herman, has the unique distinction of having been born at Harbor View Park and of making her debut in California Hall of the Pan-Pacific Exposition. "Exposition buildings extended the length of the Marina to Fillmore Street," she says, "many of them as impressive in size as the Palace of Fine Arts, but none so beautiful."

Bernard R. Maybeck's picturesquely decomposing palace and its pond provide the favorite walk of many dozens of San Franciscans, a treasured holiday memory of hundreds of tourists and a source of survival for thousands of canvasbacks, pintails and mud hens who annually drop in, like visiting firemen, on the resident swans, Canada geese, and mallard and Peking ducks.

It is a civilized, almost continental, eight-block excursion in urbanity, good at any time, season or weather. A likely place to begin is the corner of Bay and Baker Streets. Long ago a steam dummy ran along Baker taking picnickers to Grandpapa Herman's gardens, restaurant, shooting gallery and hot saltwater baths. Now from this point the walker gets a panoramic close-up of the melancholy wonder, inspired by Bröcklin's painting "The Island of the Dead," reflected in its moat. The delightful old palace, constructed in the style of the Baths of Diocletian, was intended by its architect to disintegrate gracefully.

Five city blocks of discreet town houses face on the palace grounds, but their windows are not the only ones to frame this gorgeous golden legacy from a more leisurely age. By happy happenstance, the 162-foot rotunda provides punctuation for the 40-foot roofs of the Marina and makes a middle distance landmark in the well-loved bay view for all that vast grandstand of Pacific Heights, Nob, Russian and Telegraph Hills.

As one Cow Hollow native says, "You wouldn't want more than one palace to look down on, but even people who don't feel guilty about disliking rococo architecture admit it adds something special to the perspective. And of course, when it is lighted at Christmastime, there is nothing in the city to compare with it."

Bearing west on Bay Street, the walker will discover that Lyon stops in a helio-trap for sunbathers. A footpath begins at the entrance to the colonnade, passes through a grove of weeping Lawson cypresses and picks up a macadam walk about 50 feet east near a single water-spurt, once surrounded by sculptured nymphs. It skirts the water's edge, then loops around behind the building to terminate at the starting point, Bay and Lyon, near the Golden Gate Bridge approach.

En route around the palace the walker will pass hedges, trees, lawns, an island and a peninsula, and sometimes nursemaids, courting couples, pedigreed whippets, a man displaying a white rat, well-mannered children and chronic duckfeeders. Many of the latter are members of the Palace of Fine Arts League, the enthusiasts who, with philanthropist Walter Johnson, are responsible for the building's rehabilitation. In its time the fine old palace has housed the paintings of Picasso, Mary Cassatt, Monet, Manet, and Millet, as well as tennis courts, fire engines and Boy Scouts. Now it houses the Exploratorium, a contemporary museum far from the building's original purpose, fine arts. And that's the way the plaster crumbles today.

MARINA BOULEVARD

Walking Time: A brisk half hour. **Distance:** Roughly ten city blocks. **Parking:** Great. **Available Public Transportation:** Bus 30 to Chestnut and Laguna. Bus 22 Fillmore and Marina boulevard. Return via bus 30 from Jefferson and Broderick. **Clothes:** Warm and waterproof.

To the newcomer, at Christmastime San Francisco often seems unreal and one-dimensional. As the first carol blares in Union Square the palms and fog to many become sorry substitutes for the snows of their yesteryears. The only cure when this virgin *heimweh* burgeons is to rediscover the true living giving spirit of Christmas.

There are many places in San Francisco where it can be found, but it is on the Yacht Harbor waterfront that Christmas glows most undemandingly uncommercial. Marina Boulevard has nothing to sell but the old goodwill toward men.

The walk along Marina Green is dramatic at any time or season. From Advent to Epiphany the picture windows in the town houses that border the south side of the boulevard each frame a Christmas card. Some of them are *gemütlich*-traditional. Some are stylized, decorator-designed trees, created to complement the room in which they stand. There are trees which use nothing but golden ornaments of the largest size, aluminum counterfeits of trees trimmed in icy blue or cold aquamarine, boudoir pink trees, white-on-white trees, and the polyglot popcorn- and cranberry-bedecked trees like mother used to trim.

For stunning effect, begin walking west at dusk at Laguna where it meets Marina Boulevard. Sometimes the carillon of Fort Mason, with music as twinkly as its lights, can be heard in the distance. In the foreground, Gas House Cove, enriched with small boat berths, makes a wavering moiré reflection of Alcatraz.

On the western end of the walk, the holiday lights and miniature Christmas trees in the topmasts of yawls and schooners moored on the north side of the boulevard vie with the Christmas card windows. E. J. Dollard, long-time member of the St. Francis Yacht

Club, is the father of this charming decoration project which has entranced visitors to the city each year for the last two decades.

The fine blue and gold weather of San Francisco's Decembers often bring out kite flyers, badminton players, sun bathers, dog walkers, and yachtsmen during the daytime along Marina Green. There is also a man with a war-surplus mine detector who sometimes appears at sundown to sweep the lawns for lost change and jewelry.

At twilight, they disappear. Commuters to Marin County then appear, as hectic as commuters anywhere, but looking to the walker like a serpentine of red lights meant to be part of the seasonal *lumière*. They lead the eye to the misty lights of the Golden Gate Bridge which link the wistful lights of distant hills with the Christmas lights on either hand. To the hungry of heart this unbelievable panorama creates an electrical illusion that God's in this haven and all's right with at least one little world for the nonce.

PRESIDIO WALL

Walking Time: Twenty minutes for the spry. **Distance:** Ten city blocks. **Nearby Public Transportation:** Bus 3 to Jackson and Pacific. Near Lombard Street gate of the Presidio, Van Ness bus 45, Union Street bus 41. **Available Parking:** Exceptional. **Clothing:** Warm, casual and inconspicuous.

One of the patrician walks of San Francisco, bucolic and little used, is the eastern wall of the Presidio, which runs along Lyon Street from Pacific to Francisco.

Time has been arrested here. Looking toward the bay, the walker will enjoy a contrast of wilderness on his left and of urbanity of ingrained pretensions and old hierarchies on his right. As he climbs downhill toward the tile roofs of the Marina, he may flush a skunk, a fox, a butler in shirtsleeves, or at twilight, a raccoon.

On a fine day, from the steps which begin near the dead end of Broadway, the panorama below is a magazine-cover composition in blue and gold. In the middle distance the mellow orange of the Palace of Fine Arts is echoed by the brilliant red-orange of the Golden Gate Bridge and punctuated by the masts of yachts below.

On a dull day, the wall itself is beautiful, stone topped with link fence over which vines, and sometimes roses, ramble intermittently. It is easy to look through and imagine the encampments of soldiers from the old wars.

At the outset on Broadway, where a great wrought-iron gate is sometimes open, one might picture Lt. Col. Juan Bautista de Anza, en route from Mountain Lake where his men camped in March of 1776, to Laguna Pequena, or as later San Franciscans called it, Washerwoman's Lagoon, for surely he rode along the crest to see all that he could. His pathway for many years after was part of a Presidio trail to Mission Dolores.

The first two blocks below Broadway have stone steps with benches at the landings. As the walker pauses to rest his quivering knees, he can envision the camps of later soldiers—the California Volunteers who went to the Civil War and those who went to the Spanish-American War of 1898, the Seventh California, the First Tennessee and other regiments that tented nearby. If it is a Friday, about 4 P.M., martial music wafting from the parade ground may give these musings unexpected poignancy.

The walk is steep. This is the geological feature which has preserved its charm. Once down, if the walker must climb back up, it is the last three blocks that are roughest. To return by public transportation near trail's end at the Lombard Street gate requires two transfers. If the ache in his legs is too great, a novice walker can scream for private wheels at a paystation on Lombard Street.

Steep or not, the walk is worth doing once, if only to see the lordly comity of the city's most prominent residential area. There are also surprises to be seen. The pedestrian comes upon one of these at Green Street where a little oval park makes him pause and wonder for a moment which way to turn. Within the oval there was once a spring known to the Spaniards as the Ojo de Figueroa.

Bear left. The wall takes up again after an interruption of a few villa-like houses, which seem to be within the Presidio. They stand on part of 100 *varas* of land granted in 1838 to Apolonario

Miranda. It was his wife, Juana Briones, who had a truck garden in North Beach.

You are now at one end of Cow Hollow.

Instead of cows, children seem to predominate in Cow Hollow today. The sidewalk along the wall is nineteen feet wide and the uninterrupted slope is perfect for Flexies and roller skates. Within the fence is a nursery school for Presidio children, a Scout clubhouse and a teen-center. The happy shouts are heard on both sides of the wall.

The next block, the character of the street changes to that cluster of small shops to be found near every military post.

The Lombard Street gate is guarded by two fine old cannons which once overlooked Fort Point, and a marker announcing the founding of the Presidio in 1776. Across from it on the northeast corner stands an Episcopal old people's residence, at various times the site of a plant nursery, orchard and beer garden. A block beyond, on Baker Street, the Presidio & Ferries steam dummy engine once ran to Harbor View baths.

At Chestnut Street gate, which the walker may enter, but cars cannot, the wall ends as the freeway to the Golden Gate Bridge interposes. The walker, dazed by this catapult back into the mechanized commuter stream, may wonder, "What on earth is all the rush?"

PRESIDIO

1. PRESIDIO WALL
2. LOVER'S LANE
3. EL POLIN SPRING
4. NATIONAL CEMETERY
5. MOUNTAIN LAKE PARK
6. BAKER'S BEACH
7. FORT POINT
8. GOLDEN GATE BRIDGE
9. GOLDEN GATE PROMENADE (WEST END)

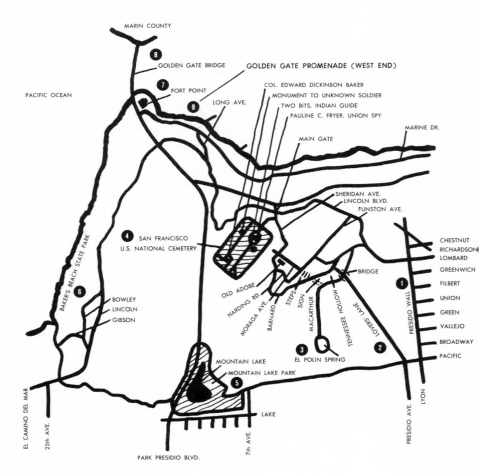

LOVER'S LANE

Walking Time: A brisk ten minutes or a leisurely half hour. **Clothes:** Comfortable shoes, sweater. **Parking:** So-so. **Available Public Transportation:** Bus 3 to Jackson and Presidio. Return via bus 45 from Lincoln Blvd. (Martinez Street through the parking lot beyond the Post Signal office takes you to the little bus station at Girard Road and Lincoln Blvd.)

Sanguine, sentimental old San Francisco has among her secret places a walk that's in the mood for love. It's a beautiful 200-year-old byway built for two through the second-act set from *A Midsummer Night's Dream,* or a sequence of full-color backgrounds for the Dunbar sofa ads.

For those of us who grew up in the unfrantic, uncrowded years, it's the semi-sylvan stroll out of memory from everyone's seventeenth summer. It's a place where you can go home again and it must be seen to be believed. So must its name, which is almost too deuced lucid to print.

The name is Lover's Lane. The Sixth Army Engineers, U.S. Army, Presidio of San Francisco, has maps identifying it by this name for the last seventy-four years and possibly longer. It is shown on the U.S. Coast Survey map of 1868 as part of the old Spanish Trail between the Presidio and Mission Dolores. How long the Indians may have used it before the Spaniards arrived is anybody's guess, for it ends near El Polin Spring.

No one remembers who were the lovers responsible for the name. Were they the Russian Rezanov and his Concha? Were they an infantryman from the First Tennessee regiment and his sweetheart, dreading seeing him go off to Manila in 1898?

Lover's Lane may not be on your map, and there are no street signs identifying it, but walkers will find it at the northwest corner of Presidio and Pacific Avenues, just inside the pedestrian gate of the Presidio. It goes as the crow flaps, along a gentle downhill grade to Tennessee Hollow where it crosses a brick footbridge and stops at Barnard Avenue, just short of the Presidio parade ground.

It exists to be walked, so bring your walking stick, tot's stroller or sweetheart some sun-drenched afternoon and try it. At the outset, look at the north side of the steep 3200 block of Pacific, which seems to be a house of a different structure, long, shingled and singularly skinny. It is not one, but a group of compatible houses abutting one another and the Presidio wall in close harmony. Bruce Porter, Willis Polk, Ernest Coxhead and Bernard Maybeck, creator of the Palace of Fine Arts, were the architects who contrived this turn-of-the-century confection.

Just inside the pedestrian gate is the high point of Lover's Lane. Look about you. This is a different world, a place of bucolic enchantment where ground squirrels scurry, songbirds sing, trilliums thrill and motes float. It is so civilized and well curried that no alien thistle nor poison oak intrudes. There is a quality of timelessness here. The stop-signs, don't-drop signs, the go-signs, the slow-signs, the billboards, electrical spillboards, neons and come-ons, the hundred million subliminal stimuli of the pushy present have been edited out of the landscape. The result is sublimely refreshing.

Lover's Lane crosses two more roads, passing a tree with a knotted rope swing and another with a tree house, a row of Georgian houses and a meadow without a swerve in course. At Tennessee Hollow, where the First Tennessee and Thirteenth Minnesota regiments camped during the Spanish-American War, it passes under an all-enveloping weeping willow tree of just the right leafiness to let sunbeams ravel through on a head of curls or a tip-tilted nose. The footbridge is the right height to sit on. At Barnard Avenue, the lane ends or loses its identity. Depending on your point of view, Lover's Lane either goes nowhere or it goes out of this world.

EL POLIN SPRING	**Walking Time:** Twenty minutes. **Distance:** About half a mile. **Nearby Public Transportation:** Bus 45 to Presidio Terminal. **Parking:** Great. **Clothes:** Warm.

"Within the Presidio reservation of San Francisco is a spring called El Polin to whose marvelous virtues were attributed the large families of the garrisons. Its existence and peculiar qualities were known to the Indians from a remote period and its fame was spread throughout California."

This provocative suggestion occurs in Volume 1 of Eldredge's *The Beginnings of San Francisco,* and is supported by a manuscript written by General Mariano Vallejo entitled *Discurso Historico,* dated 1876, which said: "It gave very good water, and experience afterward demonstrated that it has excellent and miraculous qualities. In proof of my assertion, I appeal to the families of Miramontes, Martinez, Sanchez, Soto, Briones, and others; all of whom several times had twins; and public opinion, not without reason, attributed these salutary effects to the virtues of the water of El Polin, which still exists."

Neither the files of Planned Parenthood, nor the guidebooks to San Francisco, will tell you where to find El Polin, yet Vallejo's words are valid today. The legendary spring still exists. A walker can follow the route the Spanish señoras of the garrison once walked daily, their ollas balanced on their heads.

El Polin lies, where logic says it should, about half a mile from what was once the Spanish Presidio compound. The Officers' Mess, which claims to be the oldest building in San Francisco, incorporates an adobe wall reputed to be part of the comandancia, or headquarters of the Presidio in 1776 when Lt. Col. Juan Bautista de Anza occupied it.

Beginning at the "old adobe," the walker should stroll southeast past Pershing Hall and across the Presidio street called Funston. There he will find a flight of steps which lead down to Barnard Avenue. Once across it, the walk skirts Tennessee Hollow. If you have gone far enough to find the marker which says, "In the ravines of the area southeast of this point were camped the 13th Minnesota and 1st Tennessee Volunteer regiments of infantry and other units which participated in the War with Spain," you have gone too far.

At the bottom of the steps, and just across the road, five cypress trees, whose lower trunks are painted white, lead the walker to the corner of MacArthur Avenue where a yellow sign says, "Slow, Children at Play." MacArthur is a quiet street, suburban in flavor, which lies in a valley. The homes are ranch-style, out of barracks, by General Issue. Sergeants and their families live in them. On a fair day, only a wind-eroded hillside which lies at the intersection half-way to the end of the street reveals why it is locally known as "Pneumonia Gulch."

The seeker of El Polin should continue, past hordes of children, to the end of MacArthur. There, in a road-enclosed circle of willow trees, one so old its trunk heaves out of the ground like the Loch Ness monster, is a little park with picnic tables. In its center is a cobbled reservoir, fed by two small streams. A marker proclaims: "El Polin Spring. From the spring in this clump of willow trees, the early Spanish Garrison attained its water supply. According to the Spanish legend, all maidens who drank from this spring during the full of the moon were assured of many children and eternal bliss."

Neither the City Health Department nor the Army will vouch for the purity of the water today. Maidens who go at the full of the moon drink from El Polin at their own risk. No one today seems to remember how rare is any source of eternal bliss.

NATIONAL CEMETERY

Distance: The circumnavigation of 25 acres. **Time:** Allow a morning. **Clothes:** Sober. **Public Transportation:** Bus 45 to Presidio parade ground stop. **Parking:** Good on weekdays.

There is a sad and sacred walk in San Francisco where the poignant dying fall of a bugle-note echoes through tall trees the eloquent promise that "All is well . . ."

It is a hillside stroll, dear to the Nation, valuable to all who seek perspective in this topsy-scurvy world and precious to those whom heroes leave behind. It is not a walk for the callous, nor for the "penny-wise ground-foolish," but if you feel a thrill of pride when the flag of the United States "yet waves," come some Veterans' Day or Memorial Day to the San Francisco National Cemetery. Come before 11 A.M. and let the silver-throated requiem as it sounds "Safely rest . . ." lead you through Time and to Eternity.

The National Cemetery stands, appropriately, within the Presidio, that irreplaceable preserve which, with Golden Gate

Park, has saved San Francisco from headlong congestion, the curse of less fortunate cities. Beginning at the Lombard Street gate, follow Lincoln Boulevard, part of the transcontinental Lincoln Highway, past the parade ground toward the Golden Gate Bridge. It reaches the great wrought-iron main gate of the cemetery, open from 5 A.M. till 5 P.M., at Sheridan Avenue.

Left, as you walk in, is the rostrum. Abraham Lincoln's address, made at Gettysburg in 1863, is carved on the cenotaph and enjoins us, the living, to take increased devotion to "that cause for which they gave the last full measure . . ." On the right is a little white building housing burial records and the office of the superintendent, Ernest C. (Slim) Schanze. Dispatchers think they are being ribbed when his assistant, Mr. Tom Coffin, asks for a taxicab to be sent to the cemetery, a request Mr. Coffin often makes. Mr. Schanze and his family live in the adjacent lodge.

Pause for a moment and look about. Is it a trick of the imagination, or does the sunlight seem softer here? The groping fog more protective?

Look west along the first row of marble tablets where a disproportionately boyish sandstone soldier commemorates Thomas Thompson, killed in the Spanish-American War at the age of 20 years, 7 months. "Sleep on brave Tommy and take thy rest." The inscription says, "God took thee home when He thought best." Close your eyes and the shadow armies of Lexington, Cumberland, San Pasqual, Chickamauga, Ball's Bluff, Morro Bay, Ypres, Anzio and Iwo pass the reviewing stand of the mind.

Look uphill toward the circle where Old Glory waves over the monuments. In row 46 (look along the curbstone for row numbers), near a marker that looks like a great granite bathtub, is the headstone of "Laughing Breeze," the glamorous woman "Spy of the Cumberland." The carving says, "Pauline C. Fryer, Union Spy." What it does not say on her modest tablet can be found in Harnett Thomas Kane's book, Spies of the Blue and Gray. Brevet Major Pauline Cushman Dickinson Fichtner Fryer was an actress when this word was spoken with a knowing lift of the supercili. As the first woman commissioned by the U.S. Army, Pauline is probably the great grand dame of the WAC. Her perils included capture by the Confederates, court-martial and a sentence to be hanged, alcohol, narcotics and three husbands.

Walk on past the circle to find in row 68 the grave of Two Bits, Indian Guide, dated Oct. 5, 1875. Although the burial ground did not become a national cemetery until 1884, it contained 217 known and 13 unknown dead at that time. Indians had used it as a burial place long before the Spaniards came. Two Bits, however, was brought from Ft. Klamath when a cemetery there was abandoned. Ft. Colville in Washington, Old Camp Grand in Arizona and the Modoc Lava Beds have also given up their dead for transshipment here.

Generals McDowell, Shafter, Funston and "Machinegun" Parker, the orator "Grey Eagle," as Col. Edward Dickinson Baker was known, four soldiers whose obelisk claims they were "Murdered by Strikers," and Sarah Bowman, the toast and intimate companion of more than one regiment, can all be found here. There is also a grave which contains two wives of one soldier.

Capt. Abraham Johnston, aide-de-camp to Kearny and known to historians as "Old Stove Bolts," may be one of the 408 Unknown Soldiers, whose monument is on the west side. Johnston, killed in the Battle of San Pasqual in 1846, was exhumed for shipment and his simple pine box confused with boxes of iron stove parts during a fire. A merchant who later ordered government salvage got the surprise of his life when he opened a box, expecting stove bolts, and found instead, one very faded old soldier.

On the east side, near the gate to the post chapel, is the G. H. Thomes plot of the Grand Army of the Republic. When it was dedicated in 1893, the program announced "secure in the knowledge that here" the comrades in arms and our country's defenders "may rest undisturbed by the march of local improvements, or the 'vandalism of avarice' through the generations to come."

"God is nigh" comes the lingering reprise of "Taps" and the walker, bemused, may wonder what generations of the future will do for decompression chambers.

FORT POINT

Walking Time: Allow two hours. **Distance:** About two miles round trip. **Clothes:** Sturdy shoes and a sweater. **Parking:** Good at the Golden Gate Bridge toll plaza. **Public Transportation:** Greyhound buses bound for Marin.

In his diary under the date of March 28, 1776, Fray Pedro Font wrote of Colonel Juan Bautista de Anza: "The commander decided to erect the holy cross on the extremity of the white cliff at the inner point of the entrance to the port, and we went there at 8 o'clock in the morning. We ascended a small low hill, and then entered a tableland, entirely clear, of considerable extent, and flat, with a slight slope toward the port; It must be about half a league in width and a little more in length and keeps narrowing until it ends in a white cliff. This tableland commands a most wonderful view, as from it a great part of the port is visible, with its islands and entrance, and the ocean as far as the eye can reach—even father than the Farallon Islands. The commander marked this tableland as the site of the new settlement, and the fort which is to be established at this port can be defended by musket fire, and at the distance of a musket shot, there is water for the people . . ."

Since that time, depending on your definitions, three to five forts have stood on Cantil Blanco, the white cliff. If you don't recall seeing this striking early landmark, don't despair, Cantil Blanco is no longer there. Rain leveled the first wooden fort in 1778. Wind and earthquakes took the second, horse-shoe shaped Castillo de San Joaquin, rebuilt from time to time until 1794. The U.S. Army Corps of Engineers removed Fort Winfield Scott and cut Cantil Blanco itself down to the water's edge about 50 years later.

Old Fort Point, "where never a shot was fired in anger," has what is left of Cantil Blanco as a pediment. Like the predecessors on its site, a rapidly changing world has left the old fort far behind. Today it is a quiet place, a favorite of fishermen, schoolchildren, seaswallows and sometimes of an osprey. Reaching it on foot takes some doing, but the excursion is so rich in history, and as Fr. Font described in what may be the earliest paean to a San Francisco view, the outlook so breathtaking, it is well worth the effort.

Begin this walk at the tollgate of Golden Gate Bridge. There is a shortcut footpath that leads directly to Fort Point.

Fort Point, a silent sentinel whose thick walls are joined in the little-used Flemish and English styles of bonding brick, stands at the end of the drive. Styled after Fort Sumter, it is the only fort west of the Mississippi built in the classic pattern of the 1850's. A short 100 years ago, the 127 guns installed here were considered a worthy investment.

The mastic used to roof Fort Point has created a droll footnote to military history. According to Degen's *Evolution of Fortifications,* the first cargo of mastic came from New York in a ship named the *Dashaway* at a cost of $140 per ton. En route the mastic melted in the hold. It cost the government $100 a day demurrage while the mastic was cut out.

With fine engineers' appreciation, J. B. Strauss and Clifford Paine located the Golden Gate Bridge so the fort was not displaced. Time and the ripping tides are not so kind. Five years ago it was possible to walk around the fort. Today, erosion has made it necessary to rope off the western side. Under the leadership of the Fort Point Museum Association, Fort Point became a museum and now, incorporated into the Golden Gate Recreation Area, seems safe against incursions of the motorcar. It is open daily. The Cantil Blanco Fray Font described may be gone, but from within the fort, it is still possible to see water cisterns in the floor that have been cut down into the cliff.

GOLDEN GATE BRIDGE

Walking Time: Half hour to 45 minutes each way. **Distance:** 3 miles round trip. **Clothes:** Coat, hat and gloves. **Public Transportation:** Greyhound buses bound for Marin (25 cents to toll plaza) may be boarded at Terminal and stop on Van Ness or at Fillmore and Lombard Streets.

The Golden Gate Bridge has been called a poem in steel, an Aeolian harp, an eternal rainbow and a floodgate for an avalanche of picnickers, but no one has ever called it ugly.

For artists it is as good a model as any of the bridges on the Seine. Photographers have made it the most shutter-bugged bridge in the world. Four-hundred-odd suicides have used it for a dramatic third-act curtain. Semanticists claim it is a statement.

For walkers, it is a gala walk, done for fun, eye-feasting, exercise or romance. Almost no one walks the bridge of necessity, except an occasional migrant fruitpicker. On May 27, 1937, when it was opened to pedestrians for the first time, 202,000 people flocked across it on foot. Eighteen thousand were waiting on the bridge ramps when it opened. It was one day of many-footed glory. The next day the bridge opened to the motorized insulation we call cars. Twenty-five thousand crossed.

Orr Kelly, recalling it for the *Chronicle* in 1957, wrote: "Strangely, there were twice as many pedestrians on the bridge the first day as had been expected, but far fewer cars the following day. Apparently we knew we'd only be able to walk down the center of the bridge once," he speculated. "But we knew we didn't have to hurry to drive across it. We knew it would be there for a long, long time."

The long, long time brought the picnickers that foes of the bridge feared would flood Marin glades. They brought not only their baskets but their barbecues and bedrooms. As commuters, whom one wag has described as "weekend gardeners with sex privileges," their increasing numbers bring rumbles about "second spans."

Most of the commuters and every San Francisco walker intends to cross the Golden Gate Bridge on foot. Lured by the incomparable vistas of sea, sky, bay, mountains, city, villages, islands and forts, every month about 1500 of them do it. In March of 1960 there were 993 pedestrians. In March of 1962, the number had almost doubled at 1878. This is not an accurate count, however, since children often sneak under the turnstiles at the San Francisco side and many walkers who begin at Vista Point, on the Marin side, return without going through the stiles.

The walkers en route across the bridge any fair day include families, sweethearts, serious hikers, bikers and tourists. They seem good natured, if noisy. The roar of passing cars, rather than wind singing in the cables, is what makes them shout.

To add your dime to the 1,000,000 pedestrian count since the bridge opened, begin this walk at the toll plaza on the San Francisco side. Just below it, at the Presidio view area, is a statue of Joseph B. Strauss, who "built the bridge." It does not reveal that Strauss, like so many men of grandiose plans, was Napoleon-sized.

The plaque reads, "Here at the Golden Gate is the eternal rainbow that he conceived and set to form a promise indeed that the race of man shall endure unto the ages." A more recent scientific feat, atom-splintering, has left the eulogy a little dated, but not the bridge.

Stairs lead to the bridge north of the Roundhouse (last restroom stop for an hour and a half). As you cross the bridge, look away from the stunning panorama that unreels and glance over the side-rail. The single track is for traveling workmen's scaffolding, not, unfortunately, for a monorail.

The hole in Fort Point's roof below is where a suicide went through. Bridge officials say suicides usually come by car, not on foot. South tower's famous moat, Lime Point Coast Guard Station, Fort Baker, and the unbelievably swift tide are all dramatically visible below. About midpoint on the bridge, if a ship has passed, look west. From this vantage, a ship, no matter how sleek, when quartering looks like a basset hound leaving home.

The little huts on the sidewalks house weather recording machines. Only once has weather forced cars off the bridge. It is not true that "small car warnings on the bridge" are issued when the weather is stormy, nor that you can spot the treasure ship *Rio* lying on her side. Like the legend of the ghostly hitchhiker (supposed to flag a ride at the bridge approach and disappear from your car before the span is crossed), weather and treasure are part of the mystique of the splendid span.

GOLDEN GATE PROMENADE

Time: Allow 2 hours. **Clothes:** Flat shoes, a sweater. **Parking:** Good. **Available Public Transportation:** Municipal Bus 30 to go. Golden Gate Transit bus from Marin to return.

As spectacular as any walk in the world, the Golden Gate Promenade, a 3½ mile waterside ramble from Aquatic Park to Fort

Point, is a natural escape hatch. Part of the Golden Gate National Recreation Area, newly opened October 14, 1973 by Mayor Joseph L. Alioto, this writer, and 3000 or more stalwart walkers, it follows the shoreline of San Francisco's Northern Waterfront within 50 feet of the Bay all the way. Walking west one faces the lyric sweep of the Golden Gate Bridge. Walking east, the hills and towers of San Francisco lie ahead. Either way, at your feet is sand and surf. Sail boats, fishing boats, tour boats, container ships and tankers pass within a stone's throw of the walker, yet there is a wide expanse of open space over water. Pinch me, the unbelieving mind seems to say, am I really in a city?

The entire length of the Promenade is a half day's outing one way. For the walker who would like to skim the cream of it in less time, or who isn't in shape to make the round trip, there is a fine shorter section convenient to public transportation. This is the length at the end of Marina Green between Lyon Street and Fort Point.

To make this lap of the walk, transport yourself to the end of the Number 30 bus line at Broderick and Jefferson Streets. Walk north toward the water on Broderick, through that Mediterranean village known as the Marina. It blossomed here on 50 of the 100 blocks vacated by the Panama Pacific International Exposition of 1915. At the Yacht Harbor, skirting the boats, go west two blocks to Lyon Street. This brings one alongside a handsome lane of eucalyptus trees that divides Marina Park from the Presidio. Walk exactly to the water's edge through the patio of the municipal pumping station. Here, to your surprise, there is a sidewalk across riprap. It initiates this lap of the Promenade.

Follow the water west and you will see desultory army buildings scheduled for demolition as the trail is developed with landscaping.

Abreast of Crissy Field, due to become an emergency landing field only, you reach a driftwood beach, complete with dunes, wildflowers, starfish and shells, ideal for sunbathing and surf fishing. Continue a little further and there are the trim red roofed buildings of Fort Point Coast Guard station, their frontage flanked with fine old palms. A ramp crosses the dock for the convenience of walkers on the promenade. Next landmark is the Fort Point Mine dock, often elbow to elbow with fishermen, especially when the black bass are running. Veer south around the offices of the National Park Service here and continue walking under the cliff to complete this walk at historic Fort Point, now a museum. Here the bugle calls sound as they did in the Civil War, guards wear the kepi, and a great anchor chain festoons the water's edge.

When you have dreamed away a lazy hour in this earlier century, climb the cliff behind the pediment of the Golden Gate Bridge to reach transportation back. Or better still, hoof it. The views are every bit as dramatic returning as they are coming out.

MOUNTAIN LAKE

Walking Time: Allow a morning. **Distance:** The equivalent of fourteen city blocks. **Nearby Public Transportation:** Take Sacramento bus 55 to Lake and Seventh. **Clothes:** Casual sweaters and playclothes. **Parking:** Excellent on weekdays on the avenues between Lake Street and the park.

Mountain Lake is that unexpected flash of blue fresh water that can sometimes be seen by motorists just southeast of the tunnel on the Park-Presidio Golden Gate Bridge approach. From Lake Street, to which it lends its name, Mountain Lake cannot be seen at all.

Surrounded by a well-equipped park, also named for it, Mountain Lake is very much there, however, behind the houses lining the north side of Lake Street between Seventh and Funston Avenues. It can only be explored on foot and the walk around it is a delight to all who live nearby.

The logical place to begin this walk is dead center at the end of Eighth Avenue where a flight of stone steps go up to a bench and a drinking fountain. A broad footpath runs east and west behind the houses that front on Lake Street. Bear left past the fountain, then follow the fork of the path which leads through bishop pines and leptospermum trees to a flagpole.

Pause at the flagpole. To the left is a secluded mountain meadow, full, at different times of the year, of daisies, kite-flyers, sunbathers, touch-tackle players and migrating ducks. Straight ahead is a three-sided shelter furnished with tables and benches and known locally as "The Cardhouse," where as many as ten pinochle games may be in progress. So enrapt are the old men in their games they rarely look up unless pelted, as sometimes happens, by a sack of water from the hand of a malicious boy.

The path meanders over a low, rolling ridge. At its crest spread out before you is the welcome spring-fed waterhole beside which Juan Bautista de Anza camped on March 27, 1776. A marker commemorates it in a grove of trees on the south shore. Anza called the Lake Laguna de Presidio and decided it held enough water to supply a garrison. It did.

It also partially supplied San Francisco with water between 1852 and 1870. Part of an old conduit support from the Mountain Lake Water Company can still be seen leading, like giant steps, to the water.

Yellow lupine grows along the sandy beach of the near shore. Ducks nest on the far shore, which is a U.S. Game Refuge and was twice as large before the bridge approach was built. A leg of the Presidio golf course can be seen across the water. Sometimes at water's edge is a scene reminiscent of George Bellow's famous painting, "Forty-two Kids," where boys, half hidden by the tule reeds, have contrived a raft.

From the lake the path swings up past playgrounds and tennis courts and loops around to follow the gardens of Lake Street houses. There is egress from this part of the walk at every street from Funston to Eighth. At any of them, a walker can be back on city streets in twenty paces, feeling not unlike Alice when she was disgorged from the Rabbit Hole, "eyes bright . . . finding a pleasure in simple joys, remembering her own child-life and the happy summer days."

BAKER'S BEACH

Walking Time: Allow an hour. **Distance:** Three-fourths of a mile along the beach. **Available Public Transportation:** Nineteenth Avenue bus 28. **Parking:** Good on all but the warmest days. **Clothes:** Casual. Sandals or sneakers are good for sand-walking and you probably will want a sweater.

"These have I loved," wrote Rupert Brooke, the poetic lister, "blue massing clouds . . . firm sands, /the little dulling edge of foam that browns and dwindles as the wave goes home;/ and washen stones, gay for an hour . . ."

In San Francisco, the place he is describing could be Baker's Beach. An idyllic, pristine pocket of shore that lies between Seacliff and the serpentine outcropping of Fort Point, Baker's Beach State Park is a dreamer's oasis of simple sand that restful vacations, castles in Spain, summer romances and good suntans can be built upon. Prosperous Carmel, to give but one example, before freeways overwhelmed it, parlayed a low maintenance strip of sand no more distinctive than this into a raison d'etre.

Perceptive Americans know Baker's Beach well, whether they've been there or not. Old pines and cypress shelter it beyond the dunes. Rocky cliffs define its boundaries. The soft blue hills of Point Bonita frame the front-and-center horizon. While off at stage right, that unparalleled scene-stealer, the Golden Gate Bridge, soars dramatically up and over.

Meanwhile in the foreground, what Swinburne called "the great sweet mother and lover of men, the sea" constantly renews and refreshes the firm sands, sometimes dropping treasures like driftwood, sometimes retrieving trash, like beer cans. The sea makes a good maintenance man. No grassy park could absorb the use and abuse this and other city beaches get. Sunbathers, sandwalkers, rockhounds, bass fishermen, shouting children, gamboling dogs, gulls, and rarely, a cormorant, all are accommodated here without crowding. The friendly dunes also hide the Spring Valley Pumping Station near the terminus of Lobos Creek. It once served the city and now supplies only the Presidio.

Gibson Road gives the public access to Baker's Beach. It begins at the center of Old Lincoln Boulevard, or as it is called on some maps, Bowley Street. There is no sign to mark it, but this is the only road that leads down. Walk downhill through evergreens to a parking lot which abuts the old red-brick pumping station. A gap in the chain fence gives onto the beach. Just inside are signs welcoming the public to Baker's Beach, now part of the Golden Gate National Recreation Area, advising fishermen to have permits and warning swimmers to beware the undertow and sharks. It was here, not long ago, that a young man lost his life to a killer shark, despite heroic efforts of his teen-age companion to rescue him.

Fifty years ago, if he had come at the right season, the walker would have seen clouds of blue butterflies, indigenous to these dunes, hovering over the sand verbena, beach primrose and lupine. One, Pheres Blue, is now extinct. Dr. C. Don MacNeill, lepidopterist of the Academy of Science, says the other, Xerxes Blue, has not been seen since the 1940's but someone conceivably could spot one in an obscure lupine patch.

Colonel Edward Dickinson Baker, the pioneer lawyer and senator for whom Baker's Beach is named, once lived nearby in what is now Seacliff. He lies not far away in the National Cemetery, grave 488, row 124. Lawyers gave him a commemorative headstone on Memorial Day, 1962, because he brought California into the Union.

Baker lost his best-known case to the Vigilantes, who hanged his client, gambler Charles Cora, murderer of an early San Francisco resident, William Richardson. They were afraid the persuasive "Gray Eagle" would talk him out of a conviction.

A great friend of Abraham Lincoln, Colonel Baker lost his life at the Battle of Ball's Bluff. As the walker watches the waves go home on Baker's Beach, it may seem anomalous that he should have died for the same cause that has the south in a stew today— the rights of man as modified by the color of his skin.

LAND'S END

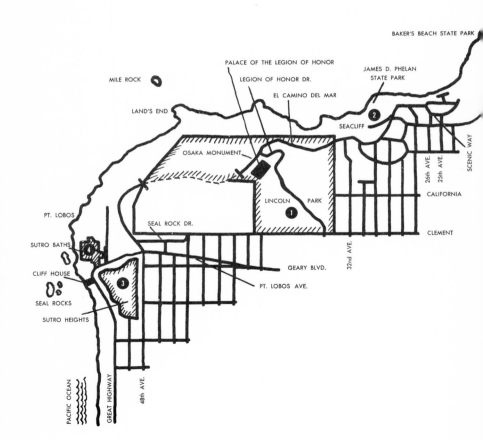

1   LINCOLN PARK   **3**   SUTRO HEIGHTS

2   SEA CLIFF   **4**   SUTRO BATHS

BAKER'S BEACH STATE PARK

MILE ROCK

PALACE OF THE LEGION OF HONOR

LEGION OF HONOR DR.

JAMES D. PHELAN
STATE PARK

EL CAMINO DEL MAR

LAND'S END

SEACLIFF

SCENIC WAY

26th AVE.
25th AVE.

OSAKA MONUMENT

LINCOLN PARK

1

CALIFORNIA

PT. LOBOS

SEAL ROCK DR.

CLEMENT

SUTRO BATHS

4

CLIFF HOUSE

3

GEARY BLVD.

32nd AVE.

SEAL ROCKS

PT. LOBOS AVE.

SUTRO HEIGHTS

PACIFIC OCEAN

GREAT HIGHWAY

48th AVE.

SEA-CLIFF

Clothes: Worldly casual with sweater. Parking: Fair. Public Transportation: Bus 28.

Seacliff perches, where its name indicates, on the brow of a sheer rock face above the sportive, slate-colored eternity we call the sea. It is a Raoul Dufy watercolor in Mediterranean pinks and whites by day, in which the utility wires are happily out of sight underground, the garages inconspicuously placed, and the demi-mansions located for neighborly view-sharing. By night it is a twinkling hill-sprinkle of lights.

Seen from aboard ship in the watery funnel between Point Lobos and Point Bonita, it is not the Golden Gate Bridge in all its glory, but modest Seacliff that melts the heart of safe homecomers, or brings to outbound passengers an unswallowable lump of the *tristesse* that follows fond farewell. Home, conceived by Madison Avenue, with an assist from slick-magazine fiction, emerges symbolically through the rose-colored glasses of heart's desire looking much like Seacliff.

Sometimes it also sounds like it.

This cliché image may have been imposed on thousands of Americans by an almost interminable radio network series called "One Man's Family," by Carleton F. Morse, which began in 1932. Seacliff was the aerie for its nest of emotional shorebirds, the Family Barbour, *genus histrionicus,* commonly known as the Much-Troubled Cliffstalkers. "I think I'll take a walk!" a member of the Barbour tribe would announce when beset by trials that would make the *Perils of Pauline* seem pale. Then off he'd go to sob along the seawall. Two generations of housewives sobbed sympathetically into the sink.

To examine this paragon of landfalls on foot, or walk off your troubles as the Barbours did, begin at the seawall where El Camino del Mar and Seacliff Avenue meet. Stroll downhill, away from the palm-studded boulevard, toward the James D. Phelan Memorial Beach State Park, an irregular crescent of sand still known to long-time residents as China Beach. Chinese fishermen once camped here. Their nightly bonfires created the myth that the beach was a private lair. It is now a teen lair.

About twice a year at dead low tide, it is possible to walk from this beach to Baker's Beach, hard by in the Presidio and separated by a steep cliff. Much of this land once belonged to Colonel Edward Dickinson Baker according to early deed records.

John Brickell opened the development of the 76 lots of Baker's property before World War I. El Camino del Mar was then West Clay Street, and 25th Avenue was a red-rock road. It was Brickell's successor, the Harry B. Allen Company, that created the sound residential planning. One member of the firm recalls that, shortly after a survey by William B. Hogue, poles were put up at various elevations to determine height restrictions.

Architectural buffs will find most of the houses of Mediterranean inspiration were designed by Appleton and Wolfard. Three residences, 9, 25 and 45 Scenic Way, designed by Willis Polk, and a handsome contemporary house at 850 El Camino del Mar, designed by Wurster, Bernardi and Emmons, are worth seeking out.

CLEMENT STREET

Time: Half a day to explore. Distance: Twelve city blocks. Clothes: Comfortable. Parking: Fair. Public Transportation: Clement bus 2.

Between the Presidio and Golden Gate Park is an area natives call the Richmond District. Newcomers often squeeze it out of verbal existence between Presidio Heights, Seacliff, West Clay Park and Park Presidio. Richmond, however, could easily represent cultural San Francisco, the world of the arts. Music, dance, drama, letters and cuisine in the city are enriched by the Richmond so effortlessly and unobtrusively that few people are aware of the dynamic community from which they emanate.

Austrians, Armenians, Hungarians, Russians, Ukrainians, Lithuanians, Czechoslovakians, and Caucasian refugees from Shanghai and Singapore have brought with them the commingled traditions of the Near East and Mittel-Europa. Clement is the street that unites them as a community. It is a street so warm, so *gemütlich,* so pleasant to shop, that first-time visitors often feel they have made a private discovery. An immediate reaction is to keep it a secret, shared only with the friend who appreciates that "superb *soujouk"* or this "unusual *presburge klipfe."*

If these foods are new to you, a walk along Clement Street can be a gastronomical adventure. Begin at Arguello, where the street itself begins. Before you have taken thirty steps, a good delicatessen beckons. Inside are Hungarian foods as lush as Zsa Zsa Gabor and every bit as tempting. Don't overeat. A few blocks farther, equally provocative Russian food is to be found at the Miniature Bakery, Restaurant & Delicatessen. Just about the time your eyes are recovering from visual engorgement, you'll reach Sixth Avenue and find Haig's Imported and Domestic Delicacies offers food from India and the Middle East hard to top this side of Iraq.

A wealth of bookstores, including Slovo, specialists in Russian language books; a printshop, where bearded publisher Henry Evans can be found at work on his handpress printing exquisite flower prints; the Jabberwock, the El Dorado and others punctuate the street. In the 900 block there are two establishments entitled The Library. One is a bookseller. The other, which looks like an elegant bookstore from without, is actually an unusual pub in which strangers can meet by telephone. Cobblers, cabinetmakers, continental candy shops, watch repairmen and pet shops are interspersed with such religious estalishments as Bahai, Shalom Center, a Christian mission for Jews, and a society of self-expression which calls itself The Outlet. Lyric instruments, from audiophone to xylophone, including lutes, kotos, samisens and possibly theorboes and hautboys, seem to be displayed in Clement Street's music shops. To perceive the extent of local music appreciation, a walker must stop at Bus Van Moving and Storage Company. Here a sign on a keyboard advises, "Children, please don't play the piano unless your name is Mozart." Presumably this goes for Schroeder, too.

Clement Street seems most exotic near Russian Easter. Then the bakeries and delicatessen blossom with high-domed pastries. The bookstores offer traditional cards. Hand decorated eggs appear in shop windows, such as Rosita Candy Co., Marion Perks or the Wagon Wheel, all proclaiming the Russian motto seldom heard in the Russia of today: *Christos voskres!* Christ is Risen!

LINCOLN PARK

Nearby Public Transportation: Clement bus 2. **Parking:** Good. **Distance:** About a mile and a half. **Time:** Alone, without digressions, allow an hour. **Clothing:** Warm for walking, sophisticated for the Legion of Honor.

Golf and culture bring more than 100,000 visitors each year to Lincoln Park, most of whom never suspect they've been through potter's field. This impressive sweep of greensward on the headlands of Point Lobos has other little known assets, including architectural incongruities, vicarious thrills and a stunning urban vista. Not the least of its enchantments is a mile-and-a-half ramble through dell and fell so well routed it interferes with no one's game.

It is a good walk, morning, evening, weekday or weekend and has its own special mystery when fog sifts vaguely through the trees, erasing time and landmarks.

Starting at Thirty-third and Clement Streets, the walker will discover a sidewalk into the park just beyond a supermarket pale. It angles past a children's playground toward the Lincoln Park clubhouse, merges briefly with a driveway and leads into a grove of trees beyond a garage. Soon it passes California Street which ends in a dramatic flight of concrete steps thoughtfully surmounted by a bench. Beyond it the walk turns into a wide footpath separating the eighteenth hole from Burke's Tennis Club. Watch for flying expletives. From this vantage the walker may observe where all's fair among those shouting love and fore.

El Camino del Mar, the street radio made famous, soon intercepts. As you cross it, look east for the glimpse of Seacliff, cuddled catlike into a coastal curve. Developer Harry B. Allen designed Seacliff so well in 1933 it still looks attractive from every angle.

Turn left and follow the roadway walk which overlooks the steep shore and leads toward Land's End. Point Bonita and the wind- and wave-shorn hills of Marin lie on the opposite shore. If he is inclined, the walker can muse on the treacheries of the sea, for this scenic funnel of coast is a notorious graveyard of ships. Probably the most romantic ship to run aground here was the legendary steamer, the *City of Rio de Janeiro,* reputedly carrying a fortune in silver.

The cliffs are also treacherous. There are paths that lead over to the eroding shore. Don't be tempted to get a closer look at Mile Rock. The sliding steeps along the shore claim several lives each year.

At the Osaka monument, turn instead to Adolph and Alma de Bretteville Spreckels' gift to San Francisco, the Palace of the Legion of Honor. A memorial to dead warriors of World Conflict I, the Legion is full of treats, including many of the works of August Rodin and the remarkable Achenbach Collection of Graphic Arts. Rodin's "Thinker," sits in the atrium. At either flanking side lawn of the building, facing a large fountain surrounded by parking, two large equestrian statues of El Cid and Joan of Arc by Anna Hyatt Huntington. It is a good walk within. Another good walk with several surprises goes around the outside of the colonnaded building.

The fountain and flagpole across from it mark the western end of the Lincoln Highway. No matter what cynics think, "The Shades," a gloomy group of nude males by Rodin, is not a commentary on transcontinental travel: it is a memorial to pioneer philanthropist Raphael Weill.

From the stone balustrade behind it, the walker can see the splendor distance lends the city. He can also see, in a nearby grove on the golf course, tangible evidence of the folly of tasteless civic endeavor. One of Dr. Henry Cogswell's hideosities, a bronze obelisk, overembellished with roses and anchors, commemorates ladies who used to bury unclaimed dead seamen here. Golfers play over thousands of pauper graves.

Another interesting remnant of old Golden Gate Cemetery stands near the first tee. Walking diagonally back toward Thirty-third and Clement from the Palace of the Legion of Honor, it can be found across the road (white lines mark the crosswalk) in a grove of trees. This is an arch from a crypt where the Chinese, or Celestials as they were called then, were deposited until their bones could make it home to China. Since a feast was part of the funeral rites, a ghoulish gang of hoboes once hung out near the Land's End railroad tunnel. In those days a local slur went, "He'd steal the victuals off a Chinaman's grave!"

LAND'S END

Walking Time: Half an hour.
Clothes: Countrified. **Parking :**
Plenty. **Public Transportation:**
Buses 2X, 18 or 2 to Point Lobos
and 48th. Seacliff bus 28. Bus 31
or 1 on 33rd Avenue to return.

Land's End sings a primal siren song to walkers. "Here I stand
beautiful beyond all expectations." It seems to say, "Come try me
at your peril."

This end to the land lies between Point Lobos and Fort Point,
where the sea and sky meet San Francisco in the old unending
conflict of wind and wave against rock. It is a wild and craggy
steep at the mouth of that drowned river canyon that has let old
Papa Sacramento River escape to the sea. The Golden Gate strait
and narrows lie below. Point Bonita and the leonine hills of Marin
lie beyond. Every year the irresistible music of challenge lures
another overbold climber or two out onto the crumbling cliffs. The
lucky ones get pulled off by helicopter. The others join Mother
Carey's chickens in the treacherous water below.

Yet there is a ramble that is safe for walkers through this
beautiful terrain. It is the old roadbed of El Camino del Mar and it
may well be the most popular dog run in the city. To find it, begin
at the corner of Point Lobos Avenue and Seal Rock Drive. Walk
north past the bell and battered bridge of the U.S. Cruiser *San
Francisco,* which forms an overlook on the sea-side of the road.
Below is the washed-out right-of-way of the old Ferries & Cliff
House R.R. High above, across the road is the Marine Lookout
Station where ships were formerly identified as they came through
the "Potato Patch," a teardrop-shaped shallow outside the gate.
Fort Miley is behind the Lookout Station.

It was on this eminence in 1774 that Fray Francisco Palou
posted his cross. In 1853 Sweeny and Baugh planted a different
kind of cross when they built the first electric telegraph in California. The companion station to which shipping arrival news was
relayed was six miles away on Telegraph Hill.

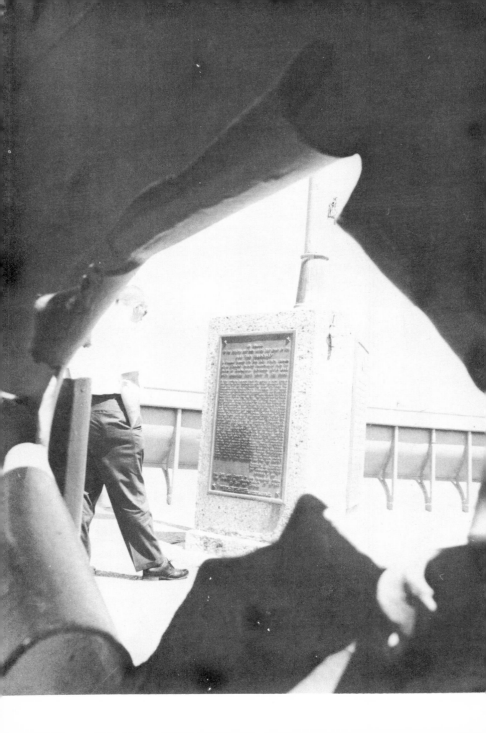

White posts wall off El Camino del Mar beyond the parking area. Here the walker and his dog come into their own, for the broad road makes a fine bright promenade between cypresses and wild flowers. Ground squirrels and rabbits play among the lupine, Indian paintbrush, wild iris, poppies and pussy willows. Occasionally a songbird warbles, or a turtle ambles out of the cattails in the gulch. Sea otters, which once were plentiful in San Francisco Bay until almost exterminated by Russian otter hunters who killed them ruthlessly for furs, have recently been reported again at Land's End. The last dens of native gray foxes have also been sighted here. Neither the otter nor fox is dangerous to man unless provoked into defending itself. The walker who keeps his eyes open may spy the wildlings of Land's End most easily at sunup and sundown.

At the first turn of the road, look through the gap in the trees toward Mile Rock Light. Many ships have run afoul in these dangerous waters and the hulks of the *Coos Bay, Lyman K. Stewart* and *Frank H. Buck* can be seen at low tide.

The shards of "Pelton's Folly," either a great fraud or a great failure, also lie on a rock between the shore and the light. Alexander Pelton, sometimes known as Ralph Starr, once built a tremendous contraption here which he claimed would "harness the tides to develop electric power." Local businessmen backed him to the known sum of $25,000 and possibly more. Three times his experimental "tide machine" was swept out to sea. One day callers at his house found clothes and furniture, and the breakfast dishes dirty in the sink, but not the inventor, his wife or son.

A berm of earth alerts the walker to the landslide which closed El Camino to auto traffic a few years ago. The slide is almost stabilized now. Since geologists have found a foothold for it, a pedestrian bridge across this gap may one day be a reality.

Bear left and follow the footpath through the gulch. Beyond another mound of earth, the walker will find El Camino passes between the Palace of the Legion of Honor and the cliffside greens of Lincoln Park Golf Course. Pause by the monument given by our Japanese sister-city, Osaka, for a superb glimpse of the Golden Gate Bridge. From this point the walker has a choice. He may cut through the park to Clement Street or continue along the shore sidewalk to Seacliff.

From the shore route, a dozen little paths, all dangerous, go downhill. The Golden Gate National Recreation Area has posted

"No Trespassing" signs wherever footing is unsure. Beyond the signs you heed the lovely but deadly lure of Land's End at your own risk.

SUTRO HEIGHTS

Walking Time: Allow an hour for exploring. **Distance:** A mile of pathway covers all the high spots. **Nearby Public Transportation:** Clement Street bus 2. **Clothing:** Headgear and a coat with buttons. **Available Parking:** Excellent.

In fashionably melancholy anapests, Swinburne, a contemporary of Adolph Sutro's, once wrote: "In the coign of the cliff between lowland and highland, / At the sea-down's edge, between windward and lea, / Walled round with rocks as an inland island, / The ghost of a garden fronts the sea."

He could have been describing Sutro Heights. Once the elaborate, overadorned home of San Francisco's philanthropic Mayor Sutro, it is now a public park where a few plaster statues disintegrate among fine old trees and battalions of rabbit-tail grass climb the granite parapet in which Sutro's ashes are hidden.

A constant and devoted corps of walkers also climbs the parapet to see the panorama from Sutro's commanding cliff. From Point Lobos and Forty-eighth Avenues, it is a gentle upward slope to the promontory which overlooks Cliff House, Point Reyes, Ocean Beach, Great Highway, Seal Rocks and what the Costanoan Indians native to the San Francisco area once called the Sundown Sea.

Pick a sunny day to walk Sutro Heights, for it is often cold and windy. Next time you go, imagine the park surrounded by a high white picket fence and at its main gate a tremendous wooden arch. In the 1880's when Sutro, best known for the tunnels which made him Last Lord of the Comstock, was in residence, a sign hung on the arch. It said the public was welcome if picnic baskets and peanuts were parked with the gatekeeper. Two recumbent lions, one with his tail twisted off, are all that remain of yesterday's glory.

Through the gate for Sunday brunch, a tradition at the mayor's salon, came President Benjamin Harrison, poet Oscar Wilde, William Jennings ("Cross of Gold") Bryan, Andrew Carnegie, and among others, Carlos Morbio, one of Sutro's grandchildren, then ten years old and hating every stultifying moment he had to spend in the banquet room. The broad promenade was known in the days of its grandeur as Palm Avenue and flanked by carpet flower beds (like the shield in front of the Conservatory in Golden Gate Park today).

East of Palm was "Old Grove" where an antler-less stag now molds among the trees. Farther along, where Diana the huntress stands, one hand gone, was a classical maze of hedge. Mrs. Harry J. Pruett, another of Sutro's grandchildren, can recall playing in it as a child. She also remembers cement dwarfs that stood by the carriage turnaround. They were probably lost at a time when, according to an amusing scholarly paper by historian Don Biggs, in the *California Historical Society Journal,* it was a good joke to say, as conversation lagged, "Let's go out to Sutro's and steal statues."

Bearing seaward, past a gnarled eucalyptus clutched in a Laocoön of ivy, the walker will discover a forlorn white gazebo, once called the Well House. It is all that was left when the mansion, conservatory, stables, watertank and watchtower were razed in 1939, after the death of Sutro's daughter, Dr. Emma Merritt, who left it as a public park to the city. Dr. Emma had accompanied Sutro in 1879 when he acquired the property for $27,000 from Samuel Tetlow, proprietor of the Bella Union Theater.

The graffiti within the gazebo justify braving its heavy connubial odor. "Toujours, Pooper," one says. Another declares, "my candles are burnt and now I die," and is signed with the sketch of an eye. Most amusing is the one that advertises, "Biondo, artist, philosopher, negativist, non-verbalist, nexus."

Long ago the lawn beyond was the setting for an outdoor performance by John Drew and Ada Rehan in *As You Like It.* It is still the setting for a reclining goatlegs called "Satyr's Dream." Satyr has lost his head.

Beyond are the spectacular view areas, each more breathtaking than the last. The southern side of the lower parapet was once called *Dolce far niente* balcony and from it dancer Beatrice Lewis fell to her death. Benches nearby are out of the wind.

Other paths lead through flowers to the foundation of the house.

One circle of lawn reveals parquet in which each tile has an optical illusion. It was the floor of the conservatory.

If the ghost of tunnelmaker Sutro sometimes laughs about San Francisco's freeway tangle as he roams about the ghost of his garden, you cannot hear it for the pounding of the surf as it whips up spindrift on the beach far below.

CLIFF HOUSE

Walking Time: Allow an hour for sauntering around exhibits. **Terrain:** A good many steps but suitable for children. **Parking:** Not bad along Merrie Way. **Public Transportation:** Clement bus 2 and Sloat bus 18.

Out at the western end of the land where the toe of Point Lobos dips into the cold water the Costanoan Indians once called the Sundown Sea, there is a walk San Franciscans save "for special."

Some of them save it especially for a winter storm, when the frightened waves run howling before a cruel whipping wind to throw themselves resoundingly against the sea stacks that are Seal Rocks. For others it is special when the troubled sky glowers and a steady rain pelts into a swirl of water boiling below. Some save it for crisp sunlit afternoon when the eye of day burns like an ingot over the distant Farallones and the combers ride majestically into shore often with surfers and "hotdoggers" on their backs.

But traditionally the Cliff House walk is to take on Sunday morning, before or after a "fizz" and breakfast or brunch. This places man, as B. F. Lloyd first said in 1876 in "Lights and Shades in San Francisco" about as near to elysian bliss as he may hope for in this world.

Pick your own favorite weather display for this walk around the restaurant whose geographical situation is so spectacular it has been a landmark by name on San Francisco maps since 1863.

Its predecessor, Seal Rock House, stands as early as 1861 on an official city map drawn by Vitis Wackrenreuder.

Historians choose up sides on two half-forgotten issues about the Cliff House. One is whether or not Seal Rock House was built in 1858 by Pioneer Sam Brannan of lumber salvaged from a ship that went aground there. The other is whether the present Cliff House incorporates part of Seal Rock House and is the fourth or fifth to stand on the site.

"As I recall, Seal Rock House was at Balboa and Great Highway," Floyd Gilman, President of Cliff House Properties, says: "We had a painting of it that was destroyed in the Sutro Bath fire."

San Franciscana buffs enjoy consulting the Junior League Historic Sites book, *Here Today*, to see what their research has disclosed on the issue. At any rate, Captain John R. Foster, a retired ocean skipper, gets the credit for naming Cliff House, while Mayor Adolph Sutro created its most fanciful architecture, a chateau-like confection built in 1896. Included within the boundaries of the Golden Gate National Recreation Area, ownership of Cliff House will one day be the people.

Begin this walk by rubbing the belly of the Japanese Temple Guard at 1090 Point Lobos Avenue. He stands beside the totem pole north of the restaurant. If you would have long life and happiness, drop in a coin for the California Society of Crippled Children. Years of massage have put a nice patina on the bronze, but haven't taken a pound off his bulge.

Walk downhill to find the restaurant. If the weather is stormy, you may want to seek warmth in the cozy Sequoia room, but to stroll the point, continue to the south end of the building. Here in a brick entryway are a few steps, leading down. If you reach a tall skinny totem pole, you have gone too far.

Go down the steps and walk around the building to see a wonderful view up and down the coast. The Seal Rocks, directly offshore, are wildlife sanctuaries. Walk on around to the north end of the building to see a statue of the Stellar seal which once abounded here.

The sea lions now breed further south at Año Nuevo Island on the San Mateo coast. If you can tear your eyes away from the seascape, notice the miniature Mission pilgrimage on this landing. For a dime, one can visit all 21 missions in miniature.

The Sky Tram, once a favorite here on the next level below,

is now gone, alas. In its station are some of the historical favorites that once amused visitors at Sutro Baths, also gone.

If the weather's bad, drop a coin into one of the slots of the Musée Méchanique, one of the best collections of mechanical music machines in the world. Gone, alas, is the notable Christopher Pinchpeck Birdman, who plays a flute. Built in 1721, he is believed to be the only automaton of this kind in the United States.

Other oddities here are a tremendous silver sculpture and Ito, the Japanese statue whose creator pulled out his own hair to supply the likeness. When you've examined the unlikely exhibits, visit the camera obscura outside. It's just what it looks like—a giant camera.

Then end this walk by returning to Point Lobos Avenue, just before it joins Great Highway. The ramp south of the giant camera leads back to the street just beyond that second tall totem pole.

WESTERN ADDITION

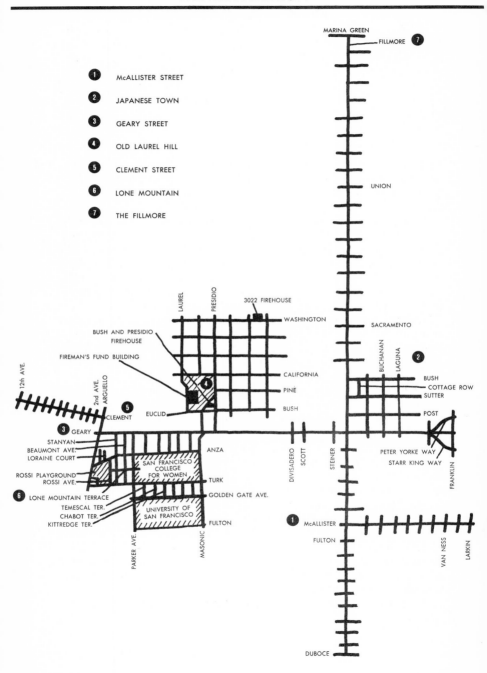

1 McALLISTER STREET

2 JAPANESE TOWN

3 GEARY STREET

4 OLD LAUREL HILL

5 CLEMENT STREET

6 LONE MOUNTAIN

7 THE FILLMORE

MARINA GREEN

FILLMORE 7

UNION

LAUREL
PRESIDIO
3022 FIREHOUSE
WASHINGTON

SACRAMENTO

BUSH AND PRESIDIO
FIREHOUSE

FIREMAN'S FUND BUILDING

BUCHANAN
LAGUNA
2

BUSH
COTTAGE ROW
SUTTER

CALIFORNIA
PINE

12h AVE.

2nd AVE.
ARGUELLO
5
CLEMENT
EUCLID

BUSH

POST

3 GEARY
STANYAN
BEAUMONT AVE.
LORAINE COURT

ANZA

DIVISADERO
SCOTT
STEINER

PETER YORKE WAY
STARR KING WAY

FRANKLIN

ROSSI PLAYGROUND
ROSSI AVE.

SAN FRANCISCO
COLLEGE
FOR WOMEN

TURK

6 LONE MOUNTAIN TERRACE
TEMESCAL TER.
CHABOT TER.
KITTREDGE TER.

GOLDEN GATE AVE.

UNIVERSITY OF
SAN FRANCISCO

FULTON

1 McALLISTER

FULTON

VAN NESS
LARKIN

PARKER AVE.
MASONIC

DUBOCE

McALLISTER STREET

Walking Time: Allow an hour or more for browsing. **Distance:** Nine city blocks. **Nearby Public Transportation:** McAllister Street bus 5. **Clothing:** Not your best. **Available Parking:** Catch as catch can.

The Fibber McGee's closet of San Francisco has long been McAllister Street. It may receive a jolt in the Western Addition redevelopment, but until it does, the walk along it is diverting indeed.

As a purely arbitrary opener, the stroller might start his walk two blocks east of Van Ness at Larkin Street. Here was the site of the old pre-fire city hall which collapsed in a mockery of civic corruption. In 1886, one of San Francisco's most dramatic killings took place nearby. The victim was a pretty fourteen-year-old schoolgirl named Mamie Kelly. Her sweetheart, an eighteen-year-old art student named Aleck Goldenson, shot her with a .32 caliber revolver. While she lay dying on an egg crate in front of a grocery store, Aleck ran to city hall and confessed. A lynch mob tried to take him from the Broadway jail a few days later. Aleck lived two years more, to die finally on a gallows on Telegraph Hill.

While nothing quite so sensational seems to be going on in it today, the present City Hall, a model of Renaissance grandeur, like its municipal neighbors, the Veterans' Auditorium Building (which houses the San Francisco Museum of Art) and the Opera House are worth more than one glance from the architectural buff. City Hall's stunning staircase has been lined with fuchsias for flower shows, carpeted in red for official functions and washed with firehoses and demonstrators during a comic-opera-size "riot."

The birth of the United Nations in 1945 happened across the street in the Veterans' Auditorium Building. An annual spectacle takes place at the Opera House on opening night when diamonds and ostentation use the building for a suitably splendid foil. This is a one-time thing to watch. By contrast, the San Francisco Museum of Art is a place so enticing art fanciers may well lose interest in walking outside of it.

At Franklin Street, McAllister reaches a visual barrier, the hideous interchange which feeds traffic into the city from a free-way. Intrepid walkers will find it can be crossed by the quick and nimble at a stoplight. Once under the freeway, the imposing municipal granite of Civic Center gives way to a podge of hodges, antique shops, junk shops and second-hand stores containing the rags, tags and stuffed bobtails of the recent past.

The neatly dressed civil servants and barristers of Civic Center, hurrying on their errands or coffee breaks a block away, live in a different world. Beyond Franklin the pace is suddenly more lei-surely. Children play on the streets among the bedsteads and pickle crocks that overflow the shops. Humanity seems warmer. There is time to laugh on the street named for a barrister called Hall McAllister, who once gambled away his home on the turn of a single card.

You will pass thirty more such shops, which house old brass, theatrical posters, sedan chairs, rare coins, religious bibelots, mon-strosities and the shards of the late Western Addition. Their owners have names like Spanish Eddie, Vincent the Welshman, Bizon, names as colorful as their stock in trade.

When the bricksom and bracksom of the Victorian age palls, stop for refreshment at the Ukraine Bakery. Here the bagels are so good they gave their name to a North Beach restaurant, the Bagel Shop, gone now like the beatniks who once frequented it. Or try the baklava. If the castoffs of McAllister don't call you back for another walk, the fancy foodstuffs will.

FILLMORE STREET

Distance: About 2 miles. Time: Two hours at a leisurely stroll. Clothes: Casual. Public Trans-portation: Bus 22. Parking: Fair.

Fillmore Street, one of the more remarkable thoroughfares draped on this lovely peninsula we call San Francisco, is like an unclasped necklace of alexandrite. It changes with a changing light.

Look at Fillmore through the rosy glasses of a young architect and it is a frayed string of tarnished Victorian beads left by the scrollsaw age. To Old San Franciscans peering at it through the lorgnette of memory, it is yesterday's market, the friendly place one shopped "After the Fire." Scan it with the hepatic eye of a planner and it is a burdensome slum-colored chain, overdue for updating. Look at it with the unswerving gaze of the sociologist to see that vanishing virtue, a neighborhood "whose strength is that it lacks pretense." Turn on the gleam of a cultural anthropologist and suddenly Fillmore is a frazzled dazzler, for along this strand are knotted twenty-one ethnic groups.

The intrepid pedestrian, who delights in the illogical juxtaposition of peoples and buildings found only in the city, can start exploring Fillmore with interest at its point of origin on Duboce. It begins in a colony of Finns. Completely extraneous to them are two distinguished buildings, the Electricians Union Building, at 55 Fillmore, and the San Francisco Funeral Service, a block away at 1 Church Street. Both are contemporary.

By the time the walker reaches the northern end of Fillmore at the Marina Green, he will have passed through settlements of Norwegians, Germans, Serbians, Slovaks, Swedes, Slovenes, Jews, Russians, Arabians, Pathans, Polynesians, Portuguese, Japanese, Koreans, Filipinos, Negroes, Montenegrans, Latins and Latin Americans, Indians and West Indians, and in deepest Pacific Heights what Gulliver called the Big-Endians and Small-Endians.

Some of the old country colonies can be spotted by a clue—a sign in another language, a shop or a *shule*. Some cannot. Perhaps the most difficult of the "shy neighborhoods," as Robert Louis Stevenson called them, to locate is the Pakhtuni community, the only one in the United States. Pakhtuni, as the Pathans call themselves, can be found east of Fillmore on Fulton Street.

Look uphill on Fulton, in the opposite direction, to see Alamo Square, where "Dutch Charlie" Duane, ballot-box stuffer, murderer and one-time chief fire engineer of the city, once fought the Vigilantes for squatter's rights to this public park.

In Fillmore's heyday, which began on April 20, 1906, while the rest of the city smoldered, great iron arches were put up along the street between Fulton and Sacramento. Overnight plate glass windows went into modest shops and for a few hectic years Fillmore gave Market Street a run for the shopper's money. Franklin Hall, which once stood at Bush and Fillmore, served as a temporary city hall. The American Theater in the 1200 block, now used as a church, is a vestige of The Chutes, a favorite amusement park in Jack London's day.

From Geary to Bush, you are "in the Mo" or "the River," as the colored population of San Francisco, whose main shopping street this section is, calls it. Informal community center is Marie's Doughnut Rack, where Judge John Bussey can be found at coffee, often with Wayne Bell or Herman Griffin, long-time Fillmore merchants who have stuck out the doldrums of redevelopment. The big white stetson on the street belongs to Wesley Johnson, sometime Texan.

Worth a detour of half a block is Cottage Row, east of Fillmore between Sutter and Bush, now being rejuvenated. The Japanese community overlaps here, but the colored roots are deeper. Nearby is the square block owned before the Gold Rush by pioneer George Washington Dennis, once a slave.

Beyond California, Fillmore climbs to Broadway and then drops precipitously into Cow Hollow, easing near Gas House Cove, names that bespeak uses of the land. The houses are more elaborate, the shops are quainter and views are stupendous.

WESTERN ADDITION

Walking Time: A brisk half hour. **Distance:** 14 city blocks. **Parking:** East of Divisadero. **Public Transportation:** Geary bus 38.

The walker who has thrown himself sensuously into the embrace of San Francisco and loves her, flaws, feather boa, pretenses and all, will find a ramble through the Western Addition offers some surprises. Geographically the Western Addition lies west of Larkin Street and its name originated when it truly was an addition to the old city limits. Now it is almost the city's center.

The cult of the Western Attrition, as one local wit calls it, has only begun. The market for elegant mementos of the doomed Victorian houses along Geary between St. Joseph's and Franklin Streets, demolished in Redevelopment Area A-2, was the first indication. The second is a growing folklore of verse, wit, song, paintings and anecdotes.

Among the brick-chippers, those mortar-stained men who came after the big destructive machines had gone, there was a singer. He had a true clear bass voice and a walker approaching could catch the words of his song before he saw the man at work in the rubble: "I got those iron-ball blues, those Cleveland wreckin' truck blues," he sang. "Those bricks on the ground, dust all around, mean and dirty iron-ball blues . . ."

The city walker who visits the renewed Western Addition to reassess the changes, as a countryman checks his acres for winter damage, may not happen on a singer, but there is much to see, including old trees newly reasserting their beauty, two new streets, Peter Yorke Way and Starr King Way, which slant off Geary into Franklin, several old streets severed, old landmarks excitingly exposed and new construction completed.

To get the lay of the land, start at Presidio and Geary, alongside what was once Calvary Cemetery. Look east, before you start walking down the street named for Col. John W. Geary, last alcalde and first mayor of San Francisco. The new Geary freeway, a broad black gash of civic plumbing which here has gone underground, leads the eye to town. Against the eastern horizon the city is revealed handsomely in panorama as it has not been for many years.

Bearing downhill past the hospitals, clinics, doctors' offices and pharmacies, and a few Victorian cottages, the walker will realize, by the time he reaches Divisadero, where Mount Zion and Sutter Towers hospitals are visible to the north, that this area is becoming a medical complex.

The park at Scott Street, across from the Benjamin Franklin high school, is Hamilton Square which has a playground and pool. It is the first of our city parks to be eroded for a freeway. Walkers who find it inaccessible from the south must either cross via a pedestrian bridge at Steiner, or if stairs are difficult for them, go yet another block out of their way to reach Raymond Kimbell Park at Fillmore, which goes over the freeway, as all these streets should.

From Steiner on, the walker can hit an open, free-swinging unencumbered stride. On one side, the Japanese Town periphery bordering Post Street looks like a life-size cardboard lithograph. Here, humanely, house-by-house rehabilitation is progressing. On the other side, contemporary efforts rise in sharp contrast. The new

St. Mary's Cathedral's great cross in the sky is the boldest massif on the horizon.

One graphic bit of Western Addition folklore stood long after all the others had gone. It was a cartoon on the north wall of a Victorian house facing the Benjamin Franklin high school, the tracery of a staircase leading up one flight to nowhere. At its ghostly landing someone had left a single poignant graffito—a large white heart.

JAPANESE TOWN

Walking Time: Ten minutes to cover the ground, half a day to browse. **Distance:** Four city blocks. **Nearby Public Transportation:** Clement bus 2, Jackson 3, Geary 38, Fillmore 22. **Clothing:** Anything suitable for town. **Parking:** Tight.

Resurging silently, slowly, surely, as the iris puts forth new shoots from old roots, Japanese Town, one of the more remarkable villages within the city of San Francisco, is preparing itself for a future season of bloom.

Planted in 1907 in the wake of the quake, uprooted, rock, stock and rainbarrel nineteen years ago in the post-Pearl Harbor hysteria, half plowed-under recently in the newly tilled fields of the Western Addition, Japanese Town has proved itself amazingly hardy.

The face it presents to the citywatcher and city walker is calm, understated, a little weary and sometimes unintentionally humorous. There are several good routes through it, but a four-block, U-shaped stroll which begins at the corner of Laguna and proceeds along Bush to Buchanan Street, then south two blocks to end at the "Little Osaka" concentration of shops on Post between Buchanan and Laguna, is a good sampler for the blandishments of this neighborhood.

Octavia, Fillmore, California and Geary Streets are the elastic boundaries of the community its own residents named Japanese Town. The entire Japanese population of San Francisco, now widely disseminated, once lived in or near it and Post is still its main street. Three churches of Buddhist persuasion, two newspapers and two movies serve it.

The homely hum of its activities includes classes in the arts of ikebana, bonsai, tea ceremony, haiku composition, wrestling, brush painting and calligraphy. And there is each year a cherry blossom festival and a midsummer day of Obon, the Japanese Hallowe'en, with masquers in kimono dancing in the street.

Superficially the neighborhood couldn't look less Japanese. The houses are mostly side-street Victorian shells, occupied hermit-crablike for want of more compatible structures. Only a sculptured shrub here, a snow-watching lantern there or a bonsai in a window, hint that the occupants come from a land where gardening is a sophisticated, thousand-year-old tradition.

The 1900 block of Bush is especially representative. Number 1909 houses the Konko Mission. Calligraphy on the doorframe and rice paper pasted in the bay windows seem oddly like contemporary jewelry on a dowdy old biddy. Next, embellished by a few unlikely clumps of bamboo, is United Enterprises, an import house. If you can wangle a pass from a decorator friend, do. The back garden has a charming pond and a choice of artifacts that would make Marco Polo's eyes bug. Hard by is a new apartment building of simple design, happily portentous of what is to come to this neighborhood since Nihon Machi, and the Japan Cultural Trade Center, with its garden, hotel and pagoda, made the transition from drawing board to Post Street.

As you walk toward Benkyo Do Confectionary at the corner of Buchanan and Sutter, look west to the YWCA at 1830 Sutter. This is a house of a different posture. It was designed by Architect Julia Morgan, best known for her work on San Simeon, and has a unique stage with an outdoor garden as part of its permanent backdrop.

The pool hall nightclubs and tempura houses are for the bold, but every walker should essay the shops. Worth exploring is N.B. Department Store, started by Shojiro Tatsuno, who lost a shop on Grant Avenue in 1906. His son carries authentic kimono, geta, zori, futon and zabuton. Across the street Honnami Taieido has folk art and the exquisite work of Hamada, Japan's outstanding potter. Soko Hardware, at Buchanan and Post, has bamboo whisks and a thousand other exotic but useful items.

Notable on Post Street are Gosha Do, the bookstore; Uoki Saki Co., where vegetables are arranged as carefully as flowers; Seiki, which has bonsai and ikebana pots; and Japan Trading Company, which has foxskin drums, kotos, and samisens.

Veterans who fell in love with cherry blossom land will not find it here, but Post Street has an ambiance, as subtle as sashimi, and sometimes, if he is not too busy, a shopkeeper will bow the customer to the door with "Sayonara."

A WALK FOR FIRE BUFFS

Distance: About 10 city blocks. **Walking Time:** Allow two hours to look at the fire apparatus. **Clothes:** Casual. **Parking:** Great on the Fireman's Fund Lot. **Public Transportation:** Clement bus 2.

"Ready the buffs!"

"Old Broderick," the first fire engine built in California, stands on Laurel Hill within sight and almost within squirting distance of the original Lone Mountain grave of its namesake, Senator David C. Broderick, duelist, late indeed of San Francisco's pioneer Empire Engine Company No. I.

The small private museum in the home office of the Fireman's Fund Insurance Companies, which treasures "Old Broderick," is open to the public only by pre-arrangement. Two firehouses are also recommended for visits as part of this excursion, the delightful old station at 3022 Washington, built in 1893, and because it houses a museum containing a number of early firefighting vehicles belonging to the city, the station shared by Engine No. 26 and Truck No. 10 companies just downhill from "Old Broderick" on Presidio at Bush.

The Fireman's Fund Museum, usually closed on weekends, is

located on the highest level of the Fireman's Fund Building, closest to the Euclid Avenue entrance. Just off Laurel is the logical place to begin this walk. For all its handsome contemporary architecture, the company is almost as old as "Broderick." Like the hand-engine, it started with the volunteer firefighters that preceded the city fire department and the word "fund" in its name derives from a profit-sharing plan originally devised to encourage volunteers.

Stroll downhill to Presidio Avenue (for some obscure reason Bush Street changes its name to Euclid at this point) to visit the fire station where the double hand-pumpers "Veteran" and "New Almaden," a steam-pumper, a hand-drawn hosereel cart, and a battery wagon are housed. There is also a "chief's buggy," a light gig whose nickname, transferred from vehicle to vehicle, is now applied to the sleek red car the fire chief drives on inspection.

The steam pumper may be the same one once bested by a handdrawn cart manned by the "Exempts," an early volunteer company whose poet laureate wrote, after a stirring contest:

The "steamer" keeps blowing her whistle and throwing
A stream from a three-cornered nozzle.
The "Exempts" in a pipe of old-fashion delight,
Then beat her five yards horizontal.

Two trucks of motorized apparatus, still in service as relief pieces, are also stored here. One has a left-hand drive that should delight vintage car fanciers. The picture collection of the late Laurent Lamanet, a long-time insurance broker in the city, is also located here while awaiting a permanent home.

The home that would offer historical continuity is the quarters of Engine Company No. 23 at 3022 Washington, an architectural and historical gem singled out for mention by John and Sally Woodbridge in their guidebook, *Buildings of the Bay Area.*

"The firehouses of San Francisco once made a wonderful catalogue of 19th century architectural invention," they have written, and they describe the hose-drying tower as "naively expressing an important building in a limited space."

Engine Company No. 23 has moved to Midtown Terrace. Buffs, whose name, incidentally, may have derived from the volunteers who slept on piles of old buffalo robes or hides slung into a corner of firehouses long ago for this purpose, will recognize this as one of the companies that fought till it dropped in 1906, San Francisco's greatest trial by fire.

LONE MOUNTAIN

Time: Allow a morning. Distance: About a mile. Clothes: Ladies wear a hat for masses at St. Ignatius. Public Transportation: Buses 31, 16X to go; 5 and 21 to return. Parking: Fair.

There is a rare, contemplative walk in San Francisco for the harried man who has wearied of the world, the flesh and the seasonal revel.

Four libraries, five chapels, a monastery, a university and a college are among its treasures—and horizons limited only by smog and the limitations of man. Perhaps nowhere else in the city reveals so well how small a remove in space, how slight a shift in attitude is needed to make an area extraordinary as does Lone Mountain.

The early Spaniards called this hill El Divisadero, the lookout or vantage point. "From the summit of this beautifully shaped hill may be obtained one of the finest and most extensive views of land and water" Frank Soulé wrote in his *Annals*.

It was for the four cemeteries at its base, however, that Lone Mountain was best known for almost a hundred years, a circumstance that led to the joking nickname "The Jesuit Act of Faith" for St. Ignatius Church when it was built in 1914. More than one skeptic asked why the biggest church in the city should be built "out in the wilderness surrounded by dead Masons?" The answer of course, is "for the Love of God." The "Act of Faith" has long since been vindicated. St. Ignatius, which celebrated its golden anniversary early in 1963, is still the biggest church, but it is now surrounded by very live students.

The last obvious vestige of the cemeteries is the San Francisco Memorial Columbarium, a mellow green-domed building at number 1, the undeniably dead end of Loraine Court. Beside the outsize country mailbox of this rich niche, once the entrance to Odd Fellows' Cemetery, is as good a place as any to begin this walk. Cross Anza Street, skirting the corner of Angelo Rossi playground, named for a former mayor of the city. About halfway along Rossi Street, you will find a gentle uphill lane called Lone Mountain Terrace. Follow this walkway three blocks uphill to Parker Avenue. It ends at the San Francisco College for

Women, the Sacred Heart school which stands on the crest of Lone Mountain. Thirty-five feet were lopped off when the school was built in 1932, replaced, the Sisters feel, by the flèche and spire on their chapel. Walk north along Parker to pick up the roadway to Underhill, the new residence for students. Follow this road to the end of a new parking lot where a stairway winds uphill through a garden, across an unexpected putting green, past temporary classrooms and up again through another garden. The path terminates alongside the Monsignor Joseph M. Gleason Library, which includes a fine collection of the photographs of Eadward Muybridge, and more than 100,000 rare books.

Before you walk down the handsome staircase, modeled on the Piazza di Spagna in Rome, look downhill to see the University of San Francisco, and beyond it, in Hayes Valley, the Golden Gate Park Panhandle. One short block of Chabot Street will bring the walker out beside the Sutro Library, Mayor Adolph Sutro's collection of rare books and incunabula, well worth a visit. Author Richard Dillon, Sutro librarian, is to be found at work here.

The opposite side of the building is the Richard A. Gleeson Library, easily confused with its Sacred Heart neighbor because of similar names. Its contemporary architecture makes a handsome contrast to St. Ignatius Church, across the mall. University of San Francisco, for many years regarded as a "streetcar college," was actually the first institution of higher learning in the city, had two downtown homes before building this spacious campus, and is best known to historians for its pioneer electrical demonstration. In 1874 Father Joseph Neri, a professor, strung three arc lamps he had invented across Market Street.

End this walk at the corner of Fulton and Parker, where there are three impressive buildings to inspect. One is the School of Law's Kendrick Hall, which has an unusual circular library. The second is the Chapel of the Carmelite Monastery of Cristo Rey. The Carmelite nuns, completely cloistered, are expatriates of Mexico and one of the most unusual spiritual enclaves in San Francisco. The historian Father John B. McGloin, Society of Jesuits, who is also their chaplain, says, "The Carmelite sisters have devoted their lives to prayer and reparation for the sins of the world." The third is ornate old St. Ignatius, which holds services at many hours and offers a respite from the world, anytime.

GOLDEN GATE PARK

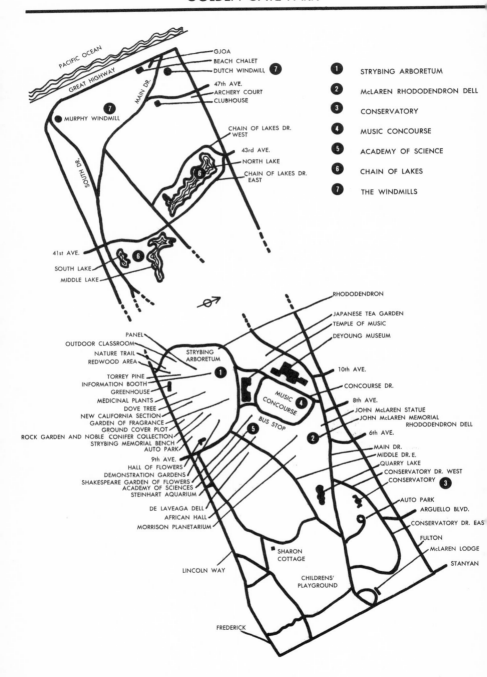

PACIFIC OCEAN
GREAT HIGHWAY

GJOA
BEACH CHALET
DUTCH WINDMILL 7
47th AVE.
ARCHERY COURT
CLUBHOUSE

MAIN DR.

7 MURPHY WINDMILL

CHAIN OF LAKES DR. WEST
43rd AVE.
NORTH LAKE
CHAIN OF LAKES DR. EAST

6

SOUTH DR.

41st AVE.
SOUTH LAKE
MIDDLE LAKE

6

1	STRYBING ARBORETUM
2	McLAREN RHODODENDRON DELL
3	CONSERVATORY
4	MUSIC CONCOURSE
5	ACADEMY OF SCIENCE
6	CHAIN OF LAKES
7	THE WINDMILLS

RHODODENDRON
JAPANESE TEA GARDEN
TEMPLE OF MUSIC
DEYOUNG MUSEUM

PANEL
OUTDOOR CLASSROOM
NATURE TRAIL
REDWOOD AREA
STRYBING ARBORETUM
10th AVE.
TORREY PINE
CONCOURSE DR.
INFORMATION BOOTH
GREENHOUSE
MEDICINAL PLANTS
8th AVE.
MUSIC CONCOURSE
4
DOVE TREE
JOHN McLAREN STATUE
NEW CALIFORNIA SECTION
JOHN McLAREN MEMORIAL
GARDEN OF FRAGRANCE
RHODODENDRON DELL
GROUND COVER PLOT
BUS STOP
ROCK GARDEN AND NOBLE CONIFER COLLECTION
6th AVE.
STRYBING MEMORIAL BENCH
5
AUTO PARK
2
9th AVE.
MAIN DR.
HALL OF FLOWERS
MIDDLE DR. E.
DEMONSTRATION GARDENS
QUARRY LAKE
SHAKESPEARE GARDEN OF FLOWERS
CONSERVATORY DR. WEST
ACADEMY OF SCIENCES
CONSERVATORY
3
STEINHART AQUARIUM
DE LAVEAGA DELL
AUTO PARK
AFRICAN HALL
ARGUELLO BLVD.
MORRISON PLANETARIUM
CONSERVATORY DR. EAS
FULTON
McLAREN LODGE
SHARON COTTAGE
STANYAN
LINCOLN WAY
CHILDRENS' PLAYGROUND
FREDERICK

MUSIC CONCOURSE

Time: Allow an afternoon. **Distance:** A mile and a half. **Clothes:** Comfortable. **Parking:** None on Sunday. **Available Public Transportation:** Bus 21 to go and bus 10 to return.

"Is there anywhere in San Francisco that would remind me of the romantic Old Vienna of my childhood?" a gentleman from Mill Valley inquired by post not long ago.

We may not have the Prater, but the Concourse in Golden Gate Park on a Sunday afternoon is for him, and for anyone else who loves musical comedy, gaiety, rococo sculpture, and culture in concentrations. Rustic McLaren Lodge at Fell and Stanyan Streets is the place to begin this stroll. At the outset, imagine a bagpipe salute, if you will, of "Scotland the Brave" or "All the Blue Bonnets are over the Border" for John McLaren, the park's most vigorous developer. Uncle John lived in the lodge like a country gentleman from 1896 until his death in 1943. More than once he and his gardeners routed squatters, or ripped up roads in the night and planted large shrubs in the roadbeds to divert misuse of the park. The tremendous cypress on the front lawn, Uncle John's Christmas tree, is decorated annually by the Park Commission, which now has its headquarters in the lodge.

Walk southwest, across Main Drive, through the funnel-shaped meadow to see the romanesque Sharon Cottage, a landmark of "Little Rec," the first park playground of its kind in the United States and, to this day, one of the most civilized. Senator William Sharon gave $60,000 in 1886 to establish the Children's Quarters, at it was then called. The lilting calliope wheeze and dashing steeds of the carousel have delighted tads ever since. Once there were also goat carts and donkeys to ride. Now a miniature farm with live animals, a cable car to climb, totem pole to ponder, swings, elaborate sliding boards and sandboxes amuse young visitors.

Beyond the parking lot, follow the road that bisects the lawn-bowling greens. A road that cuts from it beside De Laveaga dell will bring the walker out on Middle Drive at the rear of the Academy of Sciences. Go around the south side of the Academy to find an underpass for pedestrians. Echoes later, the walker will emerge near the bandstand at the head of Music Concourse. The lighthearted strains of "The Blue Danube" have resounded over the pollarded plane trees here in concert valley many a Sunday afternoon. Viennese will recognize it as a counterpark to the classic prado, prater or plaza.

Look around this sheltered, tree-laned amphitheater, a legacy from the Midwinter Fair of 1894, an exposition successfully designed by *Chronicle* publisher M. H. De Young to scotch a business recession, much as the WPA did years later. Create in the mind's eye, if you will, a lacy iron structure over the center fountain. The Electrical Tower was the name of this early space needle. On an upper level there was a restaurant, the Belvista Cafe, comparable in its time to Seattle's Eye of the Needle. Instead of a gas torch, a beam from the Electric Tower spotlighted Strawberry Hill, the island in nearby Stow Lake.

North of the concourse, the De Young Museum and the Japanese Tea Garden, both built as part of the Midwinter Fair, have survived to become better loved with each passing year. Both are good walks in themselves, so popular one must come to them at odd hours, off season, and early in the week to avoid crowds.

Worth seeking out are the Doré vase entitled "The Poem of the Vine," in front of the De Young Museum, and the wine-press in bronze across from it in the concourse. The homesick Viennese can conclude his walk a few blocks away at Fantasia Bakery on California Street, where the *linzer torte, sachar torte* and *baumkuchen* are as lush as they were in *Alt Wien.*

ACADEMY OF SCIENCES

Walking Time: Allow an hour. **Clothing:** Comfortable shoes. **Parking:** Weekends are difficult. **Time:** Academy is open daily from 10 until 5 P.M. **Public Transportation:** Monterey bus 10 takes you there. There is a fee.

The Pandora's box of science, with all its treasures and its single trouble, Truth, awaits any child in San Francisco at a compound of temple-like buildings located in Golden Gate Park and known as the California Academy of Sciences.

The collected wonders of the natural world, including stratus symbols, bush-tits, humuhumunukunukuapuaa, oryx, dik-diks, gerunuks, pterodactyls, klipspringers, zeines and an axolotl in a bottle, are all to be seen there. So is the bicolored python rock snake with the scalesome, flailsome tail, and 96,999 more reptiles, 31,000 more fish, 3,625,000 bugs, 3,000,000 mounted plants, 1,600,000 fossils and an awesome seven-figure book collection.

They could not all be looked at intelligibly by one person in one day, nor in a hundred. So, since the academy is mostly indoors, and always has something additional to see, the stroll through it has become, without question, the favorite rainy-day walk for thousands, including teachers, preachers, fathers, mothers, den mothers, stepmothers, brothers and others whose broods get broody when the ground gets wet.

It could also be called, without hesitation, the thinking man's walk. Thinking is half of what makes the academy valuable to our time and to our town, as well as what makes it fun. The other half is seeing.

To see the academy, this walk must begin at the square O-shaped court containing Robert Howard's statue of dancing whales which sometimes spouts water and has become a hallmark for the complex surrounding it. North American Hall, built in 1924, is the south arm of the O, Morrison Planetarium, completed in 1951, the north arm, and Steinhart Aquarium, which dates from 1926, the center building. An elaborate entrance was added in 1970, completing the square.

For the first-time visitor, the planetarium door is the best choice. Go through it and walk straight ahead to Lovell White

Hall. On one side of the arch is a map of the buildings (near the planetarium ticket booth). On the other side is a new blue display case labeled "Exhibit of the Month." Not long ago, it contained a collection of gastroliths. To the initiated these are the gizzard stones of dinosaurs. If it hadn't occurred to you that prehistoric beasts had crops, like chickens, you have just discovered what brings two and a half million people through these doors every year. The seven men who started the Academy of Sciences in Lewis Sloat's office, 129 Montgomery Street, in 1853 could not possibly have known that intellectual curiosity would one day make their effort outstanding, but it has.

For those who left the play *Rhinoceros* with a question, the two-horned African rhino, a gift of the late Dean Witter, financier and hunter, has the answer. It can be seen in African Hall at the terminus of Lovell White Hall.

Also at the terminus is the Alice Eastwood Hall of Botany, jutting off to the right. One everchanging exhibit of fresh California native plants carries on a tradition started by the plucky woman botanist who saved the academy's herbarium from the fire of '06. It was then located at 822 Market Street. Another popular display is the section of a giant redwood tree which has recently been enhanced by a new electrical system that shows what size the tree was in 1066 and all that.

African Hall makes a square around the auditorium and by bearing ever left the walker will be brought out into the main corridor again. Walk toward the Foucault Pendulum or "Time Ball" which swings in a constant demonstration of the rotation of the earth. It is the landmark of the Morrison Planetarium. Times for the star shows are posted on the door.

It is possible to enter the aquarium near the pendulum. A small hallway furnished with benches and a soft-drink machine gives onto the great pit swamp, where the alligators, like ambulant Gladstone bags, drowse sluggishly.

Now that the facelifting is done, the walker need not go outside and cross the court to reach North American Hall. By this time, if museum-fatigue hasn't got you, the three wonderful bookstands with their minimal-priced scientific treasures, will.

CONSERVATORY

Walking Time: An hour to see the rare plants. **Clothes:** Citified. **Parking:** Frustrating on weekends. **Public Transportation:** Monterey bus 10.

The conservatory in Golden Gate Park looks as though it had been contrived overnight of gossamer and the wings of moths. There is nothing in its mother-of-pearl fragility to suggest circuses, subdivisions or skyscraper canyons. Yet this, the most durable peri palace in San Francisco, came round the Horn in '76, is a big top of tropical plants, and coincidentally, is a direct lineal, architectural great-grandmother of the prefab unit and the curtain wall.

It is also one of the favorite walks in this city of flower-lovers and has been for 95 years. On weekends sometimes as many as a thousand people an hour stroll the narrow conservatory aisles to see its show-of-shows, changeless and everchanging, like Nature herself. The stars are exotic permanent residents (one dome-filling philodendron is easily 50 years old) and they are enhanced by a chorus of showy blooms chosen for seasonal color and custom. Lilies perform at Easter. Cyclamen and azaleas go in January 1, displaying warm reds for Chinese New Year's and Valentine's Day. Around March 16 the spring pastels of cineraria take over the stage in the foyer and west wing. These are followed in April by the plants children call "pocketbooks" or "fisherman's creel" and gardeners know as calceolaria.

To savor the wedding cake splendor of the building, a gift of pioneer James Lick, begin this walk at Main Drive facing the hollow known as Conservatory Valley, a formal promenade set about with carpet beds. One of the beds is the most famous sign in San Francisco. This is the announcement plaque, dear to the Convention Bureau, which heralds local events in posters of living flowers. Publicists beseech foreman gardner John McElvey for the space a year or more in advance. Balancing it is the new Swiss floral clock.

A much more modest sign stands just outside the conservatory entrance and announces that the public is welcome daily from 8:30 A.M. until 5 P.M. There is no charge. Doors which once opened at either end of the building have been exchanged for large clear picture windows above concrete molded to mimic exactly the glass panes set in wood nearby. Vandals and rot impelled the replacements, well worth making since a new conservatory would cost more than a million dollars.

The charming old building, patterned after one at Kew Gardens, was never cheap. Although it was a gift, the cost of putting it up was $40,000. Lord and Burnham, greenhouse manufacturers, fabricated it at Irvington on Hudson, New York, in 1875. The architect is believed to be Samuel Charles Bugbee, who owes a design debt to Joseph Paxton, creator of a tropical greenhouse in Chatsworth, England, in 1837, which had the same kind of dissectable "ridge and furrow" construction and was the prototype for the Crystal Palace. Builders are only now learning that people, like plants, can't take unobstructed glare through walls of glass.

First-time visitors to the conservatory are rarely aware of the temperature changes as they walk from room to room, but nurserymen sensitive to it can feel it if it is a point off. The croton and hibiscus rooms hover around 67°, the display room about 50°, but the pond room, which drips tropical moisture, is never permitted to be lower than 69°.

Park buffs who have discovered that the underpass in front of the Conservatory is a short cut to the Academy of Sciences may save their lives by using this route. Other underpasses there connect with the Music Concourse and the De Young Museum.

RHODODENDRON DELL

Walking Time: A leisurely hour. **Clothes:** Tweedy. **Parking:** Fair on weekdays. **Public Transportation:** Buses 10, 21, 5, 16X.

Rhododendrons are to Golden Gate Park what orchids are to debutantes, roses are to Pasadena, chrysanthemums to football or violets to sentimentalists.

There is probably more acreage devoted exclusively to this

gaudy shrub than any other plant in the park, with the possible exception of grass. The largest single concentration of rhododendrons (whose name is botanese for red-fingers) is the John McLaren Memorial Rhododendron Dell, a twenty-acre triangle across the road from the conservatory and bounded by Main Drive, Middle Drive and the Academy of Sciences.

Since rhododendrons like the same climatic conditions people prefer in a patio, a walk through the sheltered dell is pleasant anytime. When the rhododendrons are at the peak of their blooming season, usually during Lent, the walk through the dell is like a seven-reel, wide-screen, four-dimensional film in burning Vitacolor, or a gardener's fantasy of seed-catalog covers. Apricot-blossome time in Ausbeckistan or lilac time in Kew pale to pastel in comparison. First-time visitors don't quite believe it.

Newcomers to San Francisco find four plants disconcerting: The geranium, locally a wanton, but contained prissily in pots in many parts of the United States; coprosma, or mirror-plant, whose shiny green leaves seem like patent-leather stage props on first encounter; and red gum or flaming eucalyptus, a prima ballerina by any name. The fourth, and by far the most difficult to become blasé about, is the rhododendron.

Among those who never became blasé about it was John McLaren. It was soon recognized as his favorite flower. There were seven kinds of rhododendrons in the park when he arrived in 1887. Six years later there were 44 species or hybrids. Among them, and still going strong today, was the Himalayan hybrid "Countess of Sefton." Of interest to rhododendron growers, and those who garden in Latin, are three others vandals didn't get, Arboreum, Barbatum and Thompsoni.

The most widely known rhododendron, "Pink Pearl," came later, in 1912. Her name may sound like a Barbary Coast cohort of Cowboy Maggie or Pigeon-Toed Sal, but Pink Pearl is a darn nice girl. She was awarded an English ribbon of merit as long ago as 1897 and probably created the West Coast coterie of rhododendron fanciers. Pink Pearl has only one fault. Like Lolita, she takes 12 years to reach blooming age.

As much as "Uncle John" McLaren hated "stookies," as he called statues of any kind, ironically there is one of him, holding a pine cone in his hand, at the entrance of the dell, just opposite the Sixth Avenue intersection with Main Drive. This is the optimum place to begin walking the dell. Pink Pearl surrounds the statue on three sides.

Of the 500 or so species or hybrids of rhododendrons in the park to escape vandals (vandalism has been a chronic problem with new rhododendrons; many rare species which have disappeared from the park are not available in commercial nurseries), the walker should find about 50 in bloom during Easter Week. Cynthia, White Pearl, Mrs. Furnival, Hyperian, Unknown Warrior, Sarita Loderi and Van Nes Sensation are among the better known ones. Azaleas are rhododendrons and the choice rare ones can be found on Azalea Hill in the center of the dell. Quarry Lake (so named because it was the source of crushed red rock for the first park roads) has been recently cleaned and lies within the tree ferns but has no rhododendrons around it.

Park staffer Jack Spring, who caught the "rhody fever" from McLaren, thinks of the rhododendron display the park department puts into Union Square and sometimes into Macy's as an appetizer. Rhododendron dell is the banquet.

He is not to be taken literally. As long ago as 1897, Mary Elizabeth Parsons, botanist and author of *The Wild Flowers of California,* who described a native rhododendron, the Rose Bay, as "a shrub so beautiful we marvel it is not generally cultivated in gardens," warned that honey from it was reputed to be poisonous and described the leaves of the California azalea as "poisonous if eaten but not at all harmful to the touch."

STRYBING ARBORETUM

Walking Time: Allow half a day. **Distance:** One and one-half miles. **Nearby Public Transportation:** Monterery 10, Masonic 6 and Haight-Sunset 72 all stop at Ninth and Lincoln. **Clothes:** Take a sweater. **Parking:** Hopeless on weekends.

Strybing Arboretum, one of the rare, unique walks of San Francisco, is an experts' paradise in an age of expertise. From the

Tuileries to Kew, and from Kew to Kyoto, it is known in leafy circles for the number and variety of plants it can, and does, grow outdoors. In addition to plants native to our own hemisphere, the 43 acres of Strybing Arboretum successfully harbor the plants of Japan, China and the Himalayas, Burma, the Andes and Australia, New Zealand and South Africa, including those that grow on the banks of the great, gray-green, greasy Limpopo River.

The *Dravidia involucrata,* or dove tree, the *Magnolia campbelli* and the *Michelia del solpa* are but three of the rarities that bring visitors from all over the world to Strybing. This corner of the Golden Gate Park is also so beautiful, so secret and quiet, that anyone who needs to escape pressures of today may do so among the botanical treasures.

A walker could be led down Strybing's many miles of garden paths daily and make new discoveries every time. The place to start is at Ninth Avenue and Lincoln Way, where the Garden Center and Hall of Flowers is located. This building is one of the rare recent municipal structures taxpayers can enjoy without feeling their hackles rise, for it was purchased painlessly with parimutuel racing funds.

The Garden Center of San Francisco is fairly exciting itself. The Hall of Flowers (whose only resident flowers are a big raphis palm and some anthurium in a corner window planter box) is actually the auditorium of the Garden Center. (Neither should be confused with another garden center located in Oakland's Lake Merritt Park. To add to the fun there is in California a commercial Strybling nursery, a name some people misapply to Strybing Arboretum.)

Once he has hurdled the problems of identification and location, the citywalker in San Francisco will find that the handsome pink building at Ninth and Lincoln Way (designed by Appleton and Wolfard, who also did the Marina Library) is a hotbed of activity. For example, a sale of botanical rarities by Strybing Arboretum Society, and plant shows by the San Francisco Garden Club and Ikebana International, are held annually in the building, usually in the spring. Another is the San Francisco Flower Show, our county fair, formerly held in the rotunda of City Hall. It blossoms here annually the fourth week in August. Twenty of the city's garden clubs and flower societies pool their rivalries to produce the show, biggest of many held in the Garden Center, and open to exhibitors in the nine Bay Area counties.

The wrought-iron gates at the north end of the building are

the public entrance to Strybing Arboretum. Walking west within the arboretum, you will pass the Helen Russell Botanical Library and two new gardens. One, a project of the Strybing Arboretum Society and *Sunset Magazine,* is a series of demonstration gardens. The other, getting a helping hand from San Francisco Garden Club, is the Garden of Fragrance, especially for the enjoyment of blind people.

This garden, one of medicinal plants and another of California natives, were stipulated in the bequest of the late Mrs. Christian M. Strybing, who left $100,000 to create a public arboretum when she died in 1926. Helene Strybing also left the city six emeralds and a handful of rare coins. In one of our unsolved puzzles, the emeralds, appraised after banging around City Hall for a few years in a brass-bound box, turned out to be glass and the coins to be worth $48.

Following a westerly path that loops downhill twice and circles back to the main walkway, the walker will pass several exciting new plantings, most recently the Eric Walther succulent garden and the John Muir Trail. Others include the Redwood Trail at the extreme southwest corner, which has an outdoor classroom and a living laboratory of plants covering two billion years of botanical evolution. The Redwood Trail was paid for by the Hillsborough Garden Club and is worth a walk anytime, as is the new Conifer Trail nearby. Near the propagation greenhouse, purchased with contributions from many garden clubs, is a garden of medicinal plants, planted in conjunction with the University of California; a pond whose surrounding rock garden includes the Noble Collection of Dwarf Conifers, all well labeled; an oriental garden of kurume azaleas with great stone lanterns given by Mr. and Mrs. William T. Sesnon; and a California section that has a planting of darlingtonia, the pitcher plant that eats bugs.

In a city of fewer splendors, Strybing Arboretum would be celebrated loudly. Though largely unsung, the walks through it are beautiful, and if the roster of its activities sounds like every green thumb in the city is scratching here, this should not be surprising, for Strybing is everybody's garden.

CHAIN
OF LAKES

Clothing: Flat shoes, a coat. **Parking:** Great except on weekends. **Walking Time:** Fifteen minutes for the cross-country walker who hits a brisk stride. Half an hour for saunterers. **Distance:** Roughly half a mile to cross the park. **Caution:** Take a dog or a friend if you walk it at dawn. **Available Public Transportation:** Sloat bus 18 to Lincoln and 41st avenue going. McAllister bus 5 at walk's end, near 43rd Avenue. Both go to Cliff House.

"If you had to entertain Henry David Thoreau as a visiting fireman in San Francisco, where would you take him walking?" an expatriate from Boston challenged, not so long ago.

Thoreau, the first American exurbanite, was a cross-country walker, given to scrambling up schist and down shale, through dell, fen and bracken, and by his own boast, a shunpike whose direction was ever westerly.

This may sound like a large order for a contemporary city to provide, but the answer is as easy, to use a metaphor the warder of Walden Pond may have coined, as falling in a swamp. One of the choicest walks in San Francisco, richly varied in its topography and vegetation, alive with raft-building boys, nest-building mallards and other forms of wild life, is a half-mile ramble around the Chain of Lakes near the western end of Golden Gate Park.

Thoreau, who believed some wildwood is essential to every city, if only for the enrichment of the souls of its inhabitants, would be stunned to find that three adjacent ponds could be so different, but he would feel at home here. The place to begin this adventure would be the park entrance at 41st and Lincoln Way. The time to take him would be in the inspiring first silver-light of morning, when the day, new-washed in last night's fog, unfolds hopefully.

Dawn is a magical time, a time of awakening so beautiful the contemplative man on foot may find it hard to believe that bugaboos like the H-bomb, Watergate, and income tax, exist. Once he has crossed South Drive and found the gleaming little South Lake, the walker may meet a scuttling family of quail or a skunk out for a morning's stroll. Sometimes there is a raccoon tidily sponging off his breakfast under the red-berried *cotoneaster frigida* near the water's edge, or tracks to show he has been there.

On a fair day, there is always that breathtaking moment when the sun, like a tardy artist, gilds the underwings of gulls circling high overhead, long before he reaches under the trees, masterfully retouching the earth with strong, slanting golden brushstrokes.

Another roadway crosses near the Bercut Equitation Field, named for Park Commissioner Peter Bercut, well-known horseman and amateur of gardening. Walk away from it east of the cross-park road to find Middle Lake, which is looped by a path. One of the biggest eucalyptus in the park stands between South and Middle lakes.

The perceptive walker will be aware that the character of foliage changes abruptly beyond the big tree to become predominantly Oriental. At the southern end is a stand of tule reeds, which looks like a great unkempt mass of coarse hair, but makes fine cover for migrating waterfowl. Old Japanese cherry trees and camellias border the lake, interspersed with bamboo and pampas grass.

Cut catty-corner at the intersection of Main Drive and the cross-park shortcut road to find North Lake. This pond mimics the great swamps of Florida. Visitors, many of whom have been led to believe the swamp cypress, *Taxodium distichium,* exist nowhere but in the Everglades, are often startled to find the great trees, rusty looking in winter, up to their knobby knees in water. Like the three lakes, which are man-made, the swamp plantings are among the successful and long-lasting conceits of John McLaren, a thrifty man who once asked for "a hundred thousand yards of horse manure" as a birthday gift.

A nine-hole golf course and the archery field lie west of North Lake. The buffalo paddock and the dog-training field border the east side. Old leptospermum or "tea-trees," looming out of the earth like grounded dinosaurs, shield the lakeshore from these so successfully Thoreau would not, nor will the walker, feel the intrusion.

North Lake ends, usually in a great cacophony of duck conversation, near 43rd and Fulton Streets. Thoreau, a tireless man of inquiring mind, would probably want to head back into the park to have a look at the microscopic *radiolaria,* the oldest fossils in the bay area. These are to be found in the convoluted shales by Rainbow Falls, off the Main Drive, near Twentieth. Walkers who don't know schist from shinola can look, instead, for the boy-made rafts along the western shore on North Lake. After that, a transcendentalist from Boston, accustomed to breakfasting on kippers or cod, might enjoy Sunday breakfast at Cliff House. Cliff House is noted for its Ramos fizz, but it also serves both cod and salmon.

WINDMILLS

Public Transportation: Buses 18 or 5. **Parking:** Difficult on weekends. **Clothes:** Walking shoes and a sweater. **Time:** At least 30 minutes.

Few areas of San Francisco are so casually cosmopolitan as the westernmost perimeter of Golden Gate Park. It may also be the least typical half-mile ramble in the city, for its attractions include two Dutch windmills, an internationally famous Norwegian herring boat, a soccer field, an archery court and a gardener's hair shirt.

Begin this walk at Fulton and 47th Streets, bearing south. On the left, observant strollers will discover that two widely different methods of longbow handling prevail on the archery range, the formal Rounseville system of Merrie Old England and the wrist-thwanging Western method once used by Indians of the North American plains. Occasionally a man who draws the longbow with his feet, and rarely, a crossbow expert also practice here.

Near the parking area for the nine-holf golf course, which has a clubhouse where light snacks are sold, cross to Main Drive and head west toward the ocean. North Mill, which was re-landscaped recently with tulips given by the Dutch community, looms up armless in an area now called the Queen Wilhelmina Garden, on the right. An authentic copy of a Dutch mill, it was built in 1903 to pump water from subterranean streams, has 3-foot thick walls in its concrete foundation and is 75 feet high. The sails, as windmill arms are called, were used for 20 years until a more efficient electrical pump, still in use, was installed inside.

Nearby is an exercise in humility, an artificial sand dune area, which Roy Hudson, then in charge of plantings for Golden Gate Park and a long-time assistant to John McLaren, says, "we created to remind ourselves of the origins of this land."

An underpass long led the walker out near the *Gjoa,* the 47-ton schooner-rigged sloop in which Captain Roald Amundsen sailed the Northwest Passage from the Atlantic to the Pacific Ocean. After sailing down from the Arctic through the Bering Strait, the *Gjoa* anchored off Point Bonita in 1906. Even then she seemed amazingly toylike to have survived three Arctic years. Captain Amundsen presented the *Gjoa* to San Francisco on behalf of the people of Norway in 1909. Contrary to popular misinformation, the *Gjoa* did not sail into her commemorative slot. She was beached at Cliff House and brought down Great Highway on rollers. In 1972 she returned to her native Norway.

The Beach Chalet, just beyond, is leased to the McQuade post of the Veterans of Foreign Wars. It has a tremendous glassed-in dining room overlooking the ocean and murals and mosaics created by artists of the Works Progress Administration. It could easily accommodate a "restaurant in the park" for which there is increasing clamor.

Behind the chalet a walk follows the right-of-way for an old streetcar line which once ran parallel to the Great Highway esplanade. It brings the walker past a soccer field. Between October and July, the Teutonia, Mercury, Viking, Hakoah and Olympic soccer teams compete here every Sunday. Soccer is so popular in San Francisco it is also played at Balboa and Crocker-Amazon playgrounds. Of other continental sports, both polo and rugby are played at the Polo Field at Golden Gate Stadium about ten blocks east. Cricket is played at Ocean View Park in the southwest part of the city.

Just beyond the soccer field is the park sewage treatment plant which serves a thrifty double purpose, reclaiming city sewage for soil enrichment and water for irrigation. Tomato seeds and detergents are the only pollutants it cannot conquer.

Murphy's windmill, gift to the city from a prominent banker, stands in the southwest corner of the park. Two years younger than the Venus de Milo-like North mill, slightly larger and taller, it makes a picturesque counterpoint to its cousin. Coincidentally, its electrical pump moves 40,000 gallons an hour, 10,000 more than North mill.

The path will bring the walker out on Lincoln Way, jolting him back from the leisurely and exotic world behind the windblown cypresses, into the hectic present of tree-poor Sunset District.

SAN MIGUEL HILLS

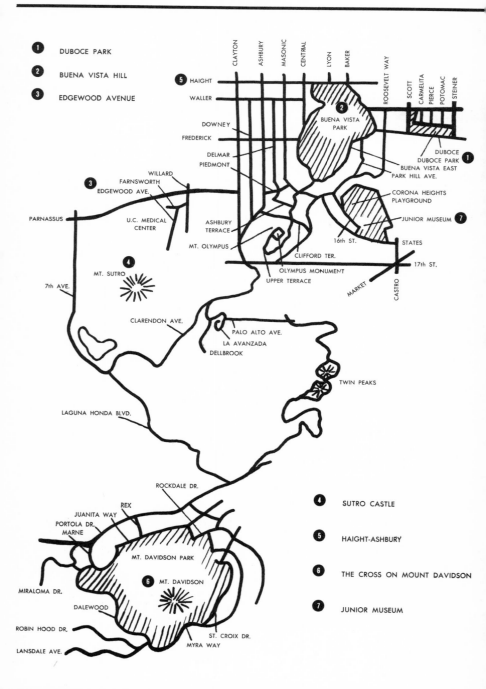

1. DUBOCE PARK
2. BUENA VISTA HILL
3. EDGEWOOD AVENUE

HAIGHT
WALLER
DOWNEY
FREDERICK
DELMAR
PIEDMONT
WILLARD
FARNSWORTH
EDGEWOOD AVE.
PARNASSUS
U.C. MEDICAL CENTER
ASHBURY TERRACE
MT. OLYMPUS
CLIFFORD TER.
OLYMPUS MONUMENT
UPPER TERRACE

CLAYTON
ASHBURY
MASONIC
CENTRAL
LYON
BAKER
ROOSEVELT WAY
SCOTT
CARMELITA
PIERCE
POTOMAC
STEINER

BUENA VISTA PARK

DUBOCE
DUBOCE PARK
BUENA VISTA EAST
PARK HILL AVE.
CORONA HEIGHTS PLAYGROUND
JUNIOR MUSEUM
16th ST.
STATES
17th ST.
MARKET
CASTRO

MT. SUTRO
7th AVE.
CLARENDON AVE.
PALO ALTO AVE.
LA AVANZADA
DELLBROOK
TWIN PEAKS
LAGUNA HONDA BLVD.

ROCKDALE DR.
REX
JUANITA WAY
PORTOLA DR.
MARNE
MT. DAVIDSON PARK
MIRALOMA DR.
MT. DAVIDSON
DALEWOOD
ROBIN HOOD DR.
ST. CROIX DR.
LANSDALE AVE.
MYRA WAY

4. SUTRO CASTLE
5. HAIGHT-ASHBURY
6. THE CROSS ON MOUNT DAVIDSON
7. JUNIOR MUSEUM

DUBOCE PARK

Walking Time: Six minutes. Available Public Transportation: N Judah streetcar to Sunset tunnel. Parking: Good. Distance: 8 blocks. Clothes: Casual.

Duboce Park, a three-block-long strip of airy green at the base of Buena Vista Hill, is a much-used neighborhood public yard, a welcome-mat ushering the N car into Sunset tunnel and the home of the Recreational Arts Building where a child can learn to play the shepherd's pipes from Robin Goodfellow or a man can master the subtleties of hypo, Ansco and synchro in his spare time. It may also be one of those unsuspected blessings the city has yet to count at full value.

City lovers who stroll around this oasis, which lies along Duboce between Scott and Steiner Streets, will find that the park and its perimeter fulfill, quite accidentally, the four conditions Jane Jacobs, nationally known critic and connoisseur of neighborhoods, requires in a district. In *The Death and Life of Great American Cities,* a book that rocked city planners off their assumptions, Mrs. Jacobs listed these conditions as multiple uses, short blocks, varied buildings and dense population. Given all four of these, she claims, "city life will get its best chances."

To see for yourself, begin this walk at the corner of Scott and Duboce. Look downhill for a panoramic urban view punctuated by the prison-like Mint on Blue Mountain. On the south is Franklin Hospital, called German Hospital until World War I. From its upper floors it is possible to see all of the Mission area, the Bay Bridge, and on a clear day, Mount Diablo.

Number 50 Scott Street, a contemporary poured-concrete structure which dominates the upper end of the park, contrasts sharply with the old Victorians, the looming guildhall-like buildings and the fat-bellied burgher-style houses that surround it on the borders of the park. The fabric of this old neighborhood, German in its origin like the hospital, is so rich the hobby photographers who come to the Photography Center need look no farther to find "typical" San Francisco architecture. Steichen, the famous photographer who spent twenty years shooting one tree and its shadow on a wall, would probably begin photographing the three houses across from the main entrance of the Recreational Arts building.

A skinny strip of the park runs along Scott Street as far as Waller, a street named for R. H. Waller, city recorder in 1851. As early as 1853 a community of five to six thousand people of Germanic origin had located in this section of the city and *The Annals of San Francisco* records a stirring *Turner Gesang Verein* celebration on May first, in that year. Not surprisingly, there is a Germania Street abutting Steiner at the foot of the park.

Walk downhill to find the entrance to the Photography Center. This hobbyist's haven has studios, darkrooms, library and meeting rooms where shutterbugs can puddle and play for a pittance. The first public recreation photo center of its kind, it has since been copied by other cities. Frederick M. Levy is the dedicated photophile who nursed the center through two temporary homes and the trauma of City Hall budget hearings to its present eminence.

Beyond the Recreational Arts Building is a much used children's playground. Notice the short streets that terminate at the park on the north side, and the houses that face it directly. These "eyes on the street," as Jane Jacobs calls them, are a greater safety factor than any police patrol. As downtown moves out Market Street, assuming Jane Jacobs' prognostications are on the right track, Duboce Park may wake up the day after tomorrow to find itself as fashionable as Telegraph Hill.

BUENA VISTA HILL

Public Transportation: Buses 43, 6, 7, 66, 71 and 72. **Clothes:** Take a sweater and wear stout shoes. **Parking:** Fair. **Walking Time:** Allow at least an hour. Go before the fog comes in.

Buena Vista, which means "good view" and not Irish Coffee, no matter what contemporary mythology would lead you to believe, is one of those descriptive names on the land left to San Francisco by the early Spaniards. The hill, park and heights of this name stand overlooking an old meandering trail between the Presidio and the Mission now paved and enveloped by the city, but traceable as Divisadero and Castro Streets.

For the intrepid walker, a climb to the crest will demonstrate that the name-bestowers did not exaggerate. The vista, when visible between the trees, is buena. More than one dusty caballero must have rested his horse on this slope, for the earliest topographical maps of the city show that, unlike many of the city's hills, trees have dressed it for many centuries. It was probably the thriving trees that impelled citizens in 1868 to set the hillcrest aside as the first plot in the San Francisco park system.

Cable cars and horse-drawn cars have also enlivened these environs in the past. The Market Street Cable Railroad built its red car Haight Street line along the northern border of the hill in 1883. The line ended at Stanyan Street where it was possible to transfer to a steam dummy that ran to Ocean Beach along Lincoln Way. The Market Street Company once made the mistake of leaving a gap between the two sets of tracks that created one of the most hilarious streetcar fights in the city's history.

One rainy Saturday night a rival line, the Omnibus Company, brought in construction crews, built 110 feet of track, connected them with a Stanyan Street terminus to which they had access and held possession by running Omnibus cars filled with construction crews, entertainers, liquid refreshments and card tables. From then on, Omnibus had 50 percent of the business out to Ocean Beach. A watcher from the slope of Buena Vista Hill could have seen the whole franchise-jumping shenanigan.

Haight Street at Baker is as good a place as any to begin this walk. At the outset begin walking on Buena Vista East uphill toward Duboce Street. A wide variety of houses lines the perimeter of the park and many of them blossomed in psychedelic colors during San Francisco's 1967 hippy heyday, "The Summer of Love."

At Duboce and Buena Vista East a Y-shaped stone staircase, one of three such sets of steps, enters the park. Veering off north is a pathway leading to two tennis courts, the stone foundation of an old WPA building, and ultimately a children's playground. To reach the crest, bear left instead and climb uphill. The stone retaining walls have ditches paved in old marble headstones from cemeteries which once stood between the park and the Presidio along Central Avenue, a street that borders Buena Vista Park on the west.

From the peak it is possible on a clear day to see Berkeley, Oakland, Yerba Buena and Treasure Island, the Bay Bridge, the Golden Gate Bridge, downtown San Francisco, the ocean and the San Miguel Hills. Sunset tunnel, all unnoticed, threads through the hill deep inside it and three large institutions, St. Joseph's Hospital, St. Joseph's College of Nursing and the St. Francis Home for Young Ladies, face on the park perimeter and enjoy its wooded wind-screen.

So does an incredible variety of wild life, including, neighbors say, a troupe of white robed jungle-drummers who sometimes come at night, tom-toms in hand, and squat on logs around a circle to play primitive percussive music.

EDGEWOOD AVENUE

Walking Time: 6 to 10 minutes. **Distance:** 2 city blocks. **Clothes:** Citified but casual. **Parking:** Fair. **Public Transportation:** Masonic bus 6.

In Edgewood Avenue, spring is a love song the plum trees sing. It bursts into a full lilting chorus of pagan pink glory one mild day with no respect to the calendar, the ground hog, the weather bureau or the vernal equinox. Behold Edgewood Avenue then and one more winter is dodo dead.

No one who sees it in bloom ever forgets this two-block street of stately old houses transmuted into timeless beauty. It is a red-carpeted aisle a bride could walk in splendor. Maurice Chevalier, slim and supple at 27, could dance down Edgewood, twirling his flat straw hat and singing, "Every leetle breeze zat I feel een my heart . . ." Pavlova in tutu would not look out of place.

"Sometimes in dreams I go back to Farnsworth Lane," a native San Franciscan who grew up nearby said, describing Edgewood in paraphrase, and she is right. Like so many of San Francisco's special secret places, there is a vantage point from which the view is unsurpassed. For Edgewood Avenue, it is Farnsworth Lane. Begin this walk on Willard, just above busy Parnassus. About seventy-five feet from the corner, Farnsworth steps slip off uphill between two truncated stone obelisks into an unexpected calm, clean greenness of trees. At the crest, a walk goes off left. Ignore it and step out onto the unpaved redrock roadbed of Farnsworth Lane, which forms a short serif at the foot of Edgewood. The hectic street and the bustling University of California Medical Center below have receded magically out of sight and sound.

Most vantages look down on a vista. Farnsworth looks up. When the *prunus pissardi* and *prunus bleiriana* are in bloom, Edgewood Avenue becomes a handwrought valentine edged in living lace and presented gracefully with love. The greenbelt begins at the southern dead-end of it, but the first-time beholder won't see the woods for the plum trees.

In or out of bloom, Edgewood, one of the few streets in the city paved in red brick, is handsome. This is no accident. A strong neighborhood association fought long ago to resist paving of any kind. The families whose homes face on Edgewood, inspired by Mrs. Meyer Levy, who still lives there, had planted the purple-leaved plum as a street tree years ago because they liked the color interplay with the natural redrock of the road, then part of a horse trail that led up into the San Miguel Hills. Red brick was the happy compromise. When the sun picks out the rich pattern of red brick in counterpoint with redder leaves or pink blossoms, no one can doubt their wisdom.

Plums, like any other fruit trees, are not an unmixed blessing. They drop fruit, attract small boys, wasps, flies and birds, and must be sprayed, pruned and picked. But every *slurb* that devours another Santa Clara orchard makes Edgewood Avenue and its special beauty more precious.

There is still a strong neighborhood association which gives a block party in the middle of the street one sunny Sunday morning each year. Edgewood has a fifty-year reputation as a "doctors' row" because of its proximity to the medical school, but there are many writers, architects, artists and businessmen who live or have lived on the street. City Comptroller Harry Ross, architect Bert Rockwell, writer Margaret Parton, columnist Elsie Robinson, novelist Agnes Danforth Hewes have been among them. So was Mrs. Philippine "Schotzie" Retenmeyer, a famous beauty and owner of the Samarkand Ice Cream Company, and Edith Bushnell, a much-beloved Poly-Hi art teacher.

They, and their neighbors, have all been people who believe that beauty, like liberty, is worth the extra effort.

MOUNT OLYMPUS

Distance: About a mile. Time: Allow a morning. Clothes: Comfortable shoes. This is a hillclimb. Parking: Fair. Transportation: Ashbury bus 33.

There is a stroll through yesterday in the heart of San Francisco. On it an average man of forty, or spry eighty, for that matter, can catch a glimpse of the good years of ball-game-size sandlots, the reassuring years of comfortable two-story houses, the gone-forever years of youth and boyhood where horizons gave on infinity.

It is to be found in the modest elegance of the old Haight-Ashbury neighborhood. "Please don't call it a district," Miss Emma Milestone, who has lived at 17 Piedmont Street since 1907, insists gently. "It is a neighborhood, one of the few in the city still worthy of the name." Miss Milestone, whose mother grew up on Rincon Hill and whose father was Captain William Milestone, skipper of the quarantine steamer *Elaine,* can recall when the neighborhood was so little populated that her dog sometimes fell into deep erosion crevasses after the winter rains. "I once saw a man fall into one," she says.

To find Piedmont Street, look for two weathered concrete columns flanked by ornamental pots of agave on Ashbury. The realtors Lyon and Hough placed these columns when they developed the area. Monroe Ashbury, like Charles H. Stanyan, A. J. Shrader, Charles Clayton and H. Beverly Cole, for whom neighborhood streets are named, was one of the surveyors who prepared in 1868 the "map of the outside lands of the City and County of San Francisco showing Reservations for Public Purposes under the

Provisions of Order No. 800." Haight Street, the other neighborhood identifier, was named either for Fletcher Haight, a prominent
pioneer lawyer, or his son Henry, once governor of California.

Walking uphill on Piedmont, usually past children playing ball,
bicycling, roller-skating or pelting pell-mell down on a Flexie flyer,
notice the handsome farmhouse at number 11. Built in the 1850's,
it was once part of a pigfarm at Frederick and Ashbury. Around
1890, a former owner moved it uphill onto rock because she
"didn't like the sand fleas down on the flat." Architect Donald J.
Clark is restoring it to its original purity for Dr. Robert Aycock.

The old brown shingled home at 1526 Masonic, upper terminus
of Piedmont, is also distinguished, although it is not easy to discern this from without. It was built in 1910 by Bernard Maybeck
for E. B. Power, a well-known attorney and has one of the most
beautiful interiors Maybeck created. A lofty cathedral ceiling, a
dining room fireplace built around a motto board from the first
wooden house in Monterey which says, "Polly Put the Kettle On,"
a great overmantel crest in blue and gold, and a garden with fine
old shrubs are among the secrets of this house. The harpsichord
music which walkers may sometimes hear from within is played by
talented Conrad Lathrop, one of two sons of Mr. and Mrs. Welland
Lathrop, who now own the unusual house.

Once you have inspected these old charmers, bear uphill on
Masonic to Upper Terrace where the observant walker will see a
forked rooftop pipe sticking out of the sidewalk, one of the oddest
pieces of "sidewalk furniture" in the city. Miss Milestone can recall
when the hillside neighbors often climbed to this corner for water
from a well here. Turn right, uphill, onto Upper Terrace, a street
that winds inward and upward to Mt. Olympus, a bowdlerism for
"Old Limpus" Hanrahan, the crippled milkman for whom the hill
is reputedly named. Continue to 240 Upper Terrace, a house which
has the peculiarity of fronting and backing on the same street. The
rear entrance, at the upper end of shortcut steps, is number 484,
and the impatient may wish to climb quickly to the little park
whose monument, "Triumph of Light," now gone, was the gift of
Adolph Sutro. It marked the geographical center of the city.

A sweeping bay view at the next curve of Upper Terrace and
another ocean view at the succeeding curve are well worth the
extra block's climb. There is a fine shortcut for walkers in the
narrow lane that comes in alongside 312 Upper Terrace and another in the stairs across from number 330. The stairs go down
to emerge at Clayton and Seventeenth.

The "bullseye" of the spiraling street, Upper Terrace, is a little round park which still has vacant lots, but not for long, if real estate billboards are any omen. Old Limpus might find the Greek names for the apartment houses well worth a chuckle.

JUNIOR MUSEUM	**Walking Time:** Allow an hour. **Clothes:** Warm coat, flat shoes. **Available Public Transportation:** Bus 43. **Parking:** Good.

"A boy's will is the wind's will," wrote Henry Wadsworth Longfellow, with unabashed sentimentality, "and the thoughts of youth are long, long thoughts." In San Francisco, the setting for this sentiment could easily be the mountaintop with the mundane name of Corona Heights.

There is nothing mundane about what a boy, or any walker bold enough to essay its craggy steeps, can see from it. Mount Diablo, Grizzly Peak, the Bay Bridge, are all in visual range. If the air were as smogfree as in the days of naturalist John Muir or agriculturist William Brewer, one might see the snow-capped Sierra.

Young eyes can also see from here the miracle in a drop of water, the riddle of the old contorted rocks, the pathway of clouds, the mystery of the trackless sea, the scintilla of galaxies in space and how earwigs mate, for this hill is also the home of a dream realized.

The dream was that of a well-known friend to local children, Josephine D. Randall, for 25 years city director of recreation. Miss Randall believed that if they are to grow up to be men of worth, boys need crags to conquer and small live unfenced creatures to observe. She led the recreation commission up the 510-foot crest of this downtown hill one visionary day in 1928 when land prices were low and soon to get lower. It was then called "Rock Hill" for a quarry and brick kiln that had been located on the southeastern slope. One of the rumors during the fire of '06 was that a volcano had erupted on a San Francisco peak. It was the brick kiln which went up in flames, spewing out molten tile the while it consumed itself. From States Street, possibly San Francisco's longest uninterrupted street, which encircles two-thirds of the hill one block below the Museum access road on Sixteenth Street, it is possible to see sections of brick masonry from this kiln still layered in the cliff like exposed geological strata. A good joke young scientists sometimes play on their contemporaries is to ask them to identify this "rare" outcropping.

The shards still lay about when the recreation commissioners examined this barren tor, but it was Miss Randall's vision of the long, long thoughts of youth that they saw. In 1941 they set aside the land, 16 acres purchased for the unbelievably low sum of $27,333, for the Junior Museum. Ten years later Josephine Randall had the fun of attending the dedication of the museum building named in her honor.

To find it, walk into Sixteenth Street where it leads off Roosevelt Way. Sixteenth curves around the hill and broadens out to accommodate the Junior Museum, a U-shaped building where children weave cloth or baskets, paint to music, make pottery, puppets, planes, masks and messes if they choose. No one says please don't handle the animals.

The museum is a good walk in itself, but to scale Corona Heights, go around behind it and look for the path that is sometimes barred with a chain. Follow this path upward. Soon it zigzags between two chain-link fences and, after a steep climb, reaches a plateau where a large barbecue pit is one of the surprises and a welcome place to rest.

Bear upwards when your knees regain resiliency to reach the peak. From it you will see that in addition to the museum, Corona Heights' blandishments include tennis courts, two small playgrounds, another picnic place, and the geological phenomenon called slickensides. The wind's will may be stronger than the walker's, but boys don't seem to mind.

MOUNT DAVIDSON

Time: An hour to walk and an hour for the service. **Clothes:** Flat heeled shoes and a warm coat. **Parking:** None, and cars are towed away on Easter to make room for walkers. **Transportation:** Bus 10 goes to the park. J, K, L, N, 5, 14, 15, 22, 25, 31, 38, 41, and 47 make transfer-point connections with 10.

For the last 200 years, a cross on a mountaintop has been the most enduring landmark of San Francisco, Ferry Building, Coit Tower, Golden Gate Bridge and other prominent latecomers notwithstanding.

It hasn't always been the same cross or the same mountaintop, but down through the years many seafarers have been grateful for it in the treacherous waters outside the Golden Gate.

The present cross, 103 feet high, made of cast concrete, lighted at night and visible for fifty miles in fair weather, surmounts Mount Davidson, elevation 938 feet, the highest peak in the city. It is reputed to be the largest cross in the Americas. By comparison, the sculptured "Christ in Concrete" of the Andes (which holds a cross aloft) is only 26 feet high, although its elevation at 13,000 is undeniably higher in the air.

It is not an easy walk up Mount Davidson, but Professor Elias T. Arnessen of San Francisco State College, who lives nearby, and his wife often walk it as a Sunday constitutional. Recently their grandson, a toddler, made the climb under his own power. On Easter, since 1923, thousands of people have climbed it in the chill of pre-dawn, sometimes in the rain, to await the sunrise sermons on the mount. They are impelled by the same conviction which has lead pilgrims to walk to Rome, to Jerusalem, to Mecca and up Fujiyama. Not all of them make it. For these, the San Francisco Council of Churches, sponsors of the annual interdenominational event, has a standby ambulance. Dean J. Wilmer Gresham of Grace Cathedral preached the first sunrise service on Mt. Davidson at the urging of his Presbyterian friend the Rev. Homer K. Pitman. In recent years ministers of five other denominations have taken part in the services under the big cross.

The first crosses on San Francisco highpoints stood, not surprisingly, near the sea. Fr. Francisco Palou planted one on Point Lobos in 1773, about where the Palace of the Legion of Honor stands today. In 1776 Ayala put his cross on Cantil Blanco, the white cliff that was leveled to make a pediment for Fort Point. Five crosses have stood on Lone Mountain, the first in 1862. On Mt. Davidson, named Blue Mountain in 1852 when Professor George Davidson, for whom it was renamed in 1911, first surveyed it, there have been four earlier crosses, all wooden. Two of them made great bonfires.

The contents of the base of the cross are typical of cornerstones except for three items, stones from the Garden of Gethsemane, water from the River Jordan and a transcript of the title to Mount Davidson from the first governor of California. The latter is a suitable memorial to the incorruptible surveyor, Davidson, whose research and careful testimony exposed as fraudulent an audacious claim by one Jose Yves Limantour to all the land south of California and west of Divisadero Streets.

Another dedicated person, Madie Brown, now curator at General Vallejo's home at Sonoma, had the foresight which made Mt. Davidson's crest a public park. See the plaque set into stone about 200 feet east of the cross for full credits.

Walkers who go for fun some sunny afternoon, rather than for faith on Easter morning, may wonder at the clumps of fern overhead growing in crotches of old cypress trees east of the cross. This species is the Leather Fern, *Polypodium souleri,* a San Francisco native that grew on the bare rocks until pioneer Adolph Sutro planted trees here, and could subsist on the cross itself, given a spore-hold.

GLEN PARK CANYON

Time: Allow an hour. **Clothes:** Rugged for dirt roads and underbrush. **Parking:** Fair. **Available Public Transportation:** Bus 10 to Chenery and Diamond Streets.

The scene is a singularly beautiful arroyo, a secluded narrow valley with a small stream rippling through it. It is moot and morsel of our Western wilderness heritage. Challenge and adventure beckon in the cliffs soaring gently off stage left. From behind a rugged rocky outcropping of the old Franciscan convoluted shales and chert in the upper right, strains of "Empty Saddles in the Old Corral" are discernible in the sound track. At any moment an Indian may appear in silhouette on the ridge. A rifle shot could ring out at any snap of a twig from Dead Man's Cave hidden in the gorse. In the foreground, the cowpoke gets off his pinto, either to water it or to kiss the sheepherder's daughter. We may never have been there, but we all remember it well.

This incomparable ravine lies, to the surprise of no one but adults, within the city of San Francisco. Its name is Glen Park Canyon. Silver Tree Day Camp occupies the greater part of its floor. To get there, go to Elk Street and turn into the dirt road just uphill from the Community Center Building.

"Ma'am, you mean you don't know where Elk Street is?" The little boy from whom I'd asked directions demanded. I shook my head. "Well, you know where Chenery is, don't you?" I shook my head. "Well, can you find Page's hardware store?" But I was already shaking my head for the third time. "I'm sorry, Ma'am," he dismissed me. "But you don't know enough for me to tell you nuthin!"

He was right. O'Shaughnessy Boulevard, as it swings down from Portola below the southern peak of Las Papas (or "The Paps" as Twin Peaks are called on the U.S. Coastal Survey map of 1869), is more apt to be within the ragged frame of reference of city-dwellers who do not live in Glen Park. The Spaniards who named the mountains, and who included the canyon in Rancho San Miguel, counted on the springs and stream that carved it to water cattle. M. M. O'Shaughnessy, the city engineer for whom the scenic swoop-the-loop thoroughfare through the canyon is named, was also impressed by this watershed. In 1912 he planned to convert it into a reservoir and dam site.

At that time high picket fences closed off the north end of the canyon so cows from Goode Brothers' dairy didn't wander onto the tracks of the San Jose railroad. Long-time resident Sylvia Anderson of 1313 Bosworth Street can remember when her children chased cows off the lawn. "We bought milk for 5 cents a quart," she recalls.

O'Shaughnessy Boulevard becomes Bosworth Street at its lower end. Elk Street veers from it by a baseball diamond. Three large stone arches at this corner once marked the entrance to a private picnic grove, dance pavilion and zoo, operated by a developer when the property was owned by the Crocker estate. The Glen Park Community Center Building, a project for which the neighborhood had assistance from Josephine Randall, long-time recreation director, now stands on the site of the pavilion.

Beyond the Community Center, on either side of the creek, the trail leads to a new Silver Tree Camp Building. Look uphill on the east side when you reach the first campfire circle to see a hole in the rocks known locally as Devil's Cave. Dead Man's Cave, reputed to have been used by Russian smugglers, Mexican rustlers, Confederate pirates and possibly the distillers of a particularly potent brand of redeye known as Panther's Piss, is farther along in the canyon, well hidden in poison oak on the south face. In the verbal history of the neighborhood, the Russian smugglers are supposed to have been hanged on nearby Gold Mine Hill.

Now instead of a gallows, the structures looming on the high horizon are part of a redevelopment project known as Diamond Heights. There are also some split-levels, genus *Eichlerii urbanicus*. No beast lows. The last cayuse to drink from the great oblong water trough uphill from Silver Tree has long since become a ghost rider in the sky.

MISSION DOLORES

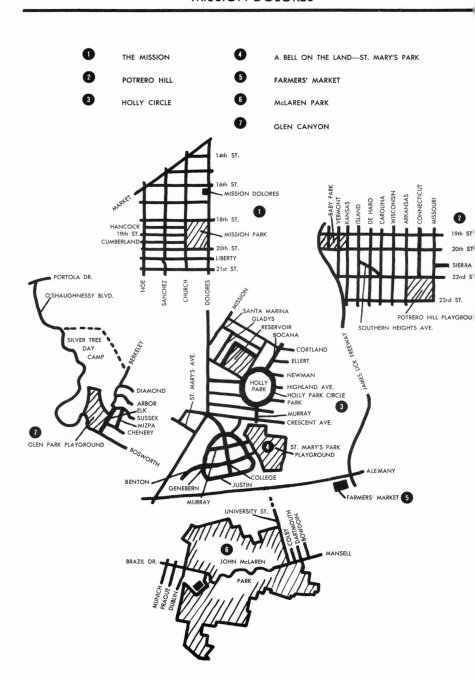

1. THE MISSION
2. POTRERO HILL
3. HOLLY CIRCLE
4. A BELL ON THE LAND—ST. MARY'S PARK
5. FARMERS' MARKET
6. McLAREN PARK
7. GLEN CANYON

MISSION DOLORES

Walking Time: Half a day. **Distance:** Five city blocks. **Nearby Public Transportation:** K, L, M, and N streetcars on Market Street. **Clothes:** Ladies should take a headcovering. **Parking:** Not bad along Dolores Street.

Mission San Francisco de Asis, or, as we commonly miscall it, Mission Dolores, is the local spot natives of San Francisco intend to visit, but don't.

Yet the indomitable old mission, little changed since it settled in like a mother hen in 1782 on what has since become the corner of Sixteenth and Dolores Streets, is one of the things tourists come to see. The walk to and around it is pleasant and strangely satisfying. For those who will risk being mistaken for a tourist, the mission has more to tell than any other building in town simply because it has been here so long.

To get the full flavor, the walker should know that the mission is one in a chain of 21 missions established by the Franciscans along the California coast from San Diego to Sonoma. Padre Junipero Serra established the first one, San Diego de Alcala, July 16, 1769. A Mexican congressional act in 1833 ordered all the missions secularized, and for years thereafter they lay in various states of disrepair. Title to the land and buildings of Mission Dolores finally returned to the Catholic Church in 1860.

For the uninformed, it is enough to know that although the Spanish captains and kings have departed long since, you can still hear the same mass next door at the Basilica that Fr. Francisco Palou, founder of the local mission, celebrated on the site June 29, 1776.

As he begins this walk at the corner of Market and Dolores Streets, with barely a glance at the ugly Mint building, a monolithic governmental monument to monumental government, the walker should look downhill along the pleasant row of palms, centered on the grassy boulevard of Dolores. With the exception of the Mission, its satellites, and nearby Mission Park, Dolores is lined with modest flats, churches and houses, some Victorian, some contemporary.

There was a time when this was a little rural valley with cattle grazing near Laguna de la Nuestra Señora de Dolores, a lake which stood where Mission high school now stands, and gave the mission its misnomer. There was a later time when the old Plank Road, now Mission Street, linked the mission settlement and the growing town of San Francisco. Once the San Francisco and San Jose Railroad huffed through this valley. Finally the town simply enveloped it.

The walker may surprise one of the faithful placing flowers before the Lady of the Wayside shrine in the mission wall, but if he has visited other missions in the chain along El Camino Real, he will soon realize that Mission Dolores looks very different. For one thing, it is almost overshadowed by the neighboring complex of sympathetic institutions.

A twenty-five cent donation is requested for the preservation fund in return for the privilege of browsing the mission and its cemetery. It's a good twenty-five cents worth. The mission is an excellent museum, with some unexpected goodies within, including well-illustrated handbooks for the serious historian. Some of the victims of the Vigilantes are in the graveyard. It is reassuring too, to find William A. Leidesdorff, San Francisco half-caste pioneer, buried here, now that creeping intolerance is once again abroad in the land.

Two bits, to use a term that is reputed to have originated in San Francisco in 1849 when the mission was already old, is little enough to pay to step almost 200 years back in time and savor vicariously for a few precious moments the peace and measured pace of a leisurely world foregone. Mission Park, two blocks south on Dolores, is a pleasant place to pause before rushing headlong back into today.

POTRERO HILL

Walking Time: A leisurely hour. **Distance:** Half a mile. **Clothes:** Walking shoes. Be prepared to shed your sweater. **Available Public Transportation:** Southern Heights bus 53 to Vermont and Twentieth. Pick up same bus at Missouri and Twentieth to return. **Available Parking:** Plenty.

Potrero Hill, an isolated country-town populated by artists, non-conformists and Russian émigrés of the Molokani sect, lies roughly equidistant with Pacific Heights from Union Square in Space and with the McKinley administration in Time.

The torrential James Lick Skyway, also called the "bloody Bayshore," surges against Potrero Hill on the west. A clanging, chugging, huffing, pounding sea of heavy industry maroons its other boundaries. High above this turmoil the Potrero hilltop community of cottages, punctuated with a few new apartments, enjoys one of the most dramatic bay views, basks drowsily in the sun, often while the rest of the city shivers, and observes rural, pre-Revolutionary Russian customs unperturbed.

The walker may find the views and warmth of the crest, once called "Scotch Hill," almost anytime. Vestiges of old Russia he will come upon by chance and recognize only if he knows what he is seeing.

A good place to begin looking is Twentieth and Vermont Streets by the scrap of green local residents have nicknamed "Baby Park." Look west to see a superb cityscape with San Francisco General Hospital in the foreground dominated by Twin Peaks, sometimes clutched in the fog formation known as "the Hand of God."

South of the park is the "wiggly block" of Vermont which snakes like the famous curlicue on Lombard. Bear east instead along Twentieth to De Haro Street, named for Alcalde Francisco de Haro who held the Spanish landgrant known as Potrero de San Francisco or Potrero Nuevo—"new grazing ground." He died of grief, early accounts say, after his twin sons were slain pointlessly by Kit Carson on the orders of General Frémont.

Walking south to Southern Heights Avenue you will pass at 953 De Haro the Potrero Hill Neighborhood Center, a United Crusade agency built in 1908 just after the Molokans established themselves here. Often the old Russian men of the community sit on benches in front, cracking sunflower seeds, and it is here, in starched white aprons, their heads covered as their religion requires, that the ladies linger after church services. Southern Heights cuts diagonally to Carolina where the Molokans or First Russian Christian Church can be seen downhill at number 841. The church is austere and has a kitchen at the rear where fancy piroshki are prepared for wedding feasts. Funeral processions, which once went to Colma on foot, also begin here. Formerly the casket was carried on the shoulders of friends as the procession retraced the deceased's path of lifetime habit. Behind many of the cottages nearby are "banya," the Russian steam baths, but the walker will have difficulty spotting one.

The cottage at Carolina and Twenty-second is occupied by a caretaker for the adjacent reservoir. The greensward at the end of Twenty-second is the Potrero Hill playground. Below it are housing projects and a tunnel that goes under the hill at Sierra and emerges at Nineteenth and Arkansas. "We played in the tunnel as children," Martha Pavloff, 709 Carolina Street, says, "and flattened against the wall when trains went through."

Going downhill on Wisconsin the walker will pass the homes of many artists, sculptors and writers, among them Ruth Cravath, Lucy Coons, and in the eyecatching Victorian, poet Lawrence Ferlinghetti. Henri Marie-Rose, Saul Padover and others live nearby. The efforts of Marian the Librarian, as Mrs. Fred W. Thomas of the Potrero Public Library, 1616 Twentieth Street, is known, have made them welcome with an annual spring art show which has no judges, no jury and no prizes.

Across the street Dr. George Roth, a general practitioner, tells time by the Equitable Building clock through the library windows. To get a gull's eye view of downtown, go in the library.

Twentieth Street toward Missouri is the hill's shopping district. The babushkas, or headshawls, worn by many older women here are a reminder that, as Carl Sandburg wrote, "America was promises." Today, when half of the world has lost the privilege, it is reassuring to recall that freedom of worship, one of America's great promises, is kept in good faith in San Francisco.

HOLLY PARK

Time: Allow an hour. **Clothes:** Windproof for the hilltop. **Parking:** Great. **Public Transportation:** Buses 9, 10, 26 and 27.

"Only the dead know Brooklyn," Thomas Wolfe once wrote. If he had chosen San Francisco rather than New York as his subject, he might have written, "Only the dead know Bernal." Bernal, like Brooklyn, has its lows and its Heights.

Like so much of the 22 square miles of the city which lie southeast of Jasper O'Farrell's exasperating diagonal called Market Street, Bernal Heights is a world apart. To see why, and to understand what "the dead know," come some balmy afternoon and walk in Holly Park.

An historical place to begin this walk would have been at Cortland and San Bruno Avenues where Don Jose Cornelio Bernal, for whose Spanish grantee family Bernal Heights is named, once built a home for his daughter and her Pennsylvanian husband, William Henry Barker. After her death, Isaac Stone bought the property from Barker, used much of it for grazing his dairy cattle, added a lake and a garden and made it one of the local showplaces during the later 1800's. Now the Bayshore Dreadway makes it too dangerous to venture onto the Bernal-Barker-Stone site. Out of prudence, begin this walk at Cortland and Elsie Streets. Dairy farms that once dotted this area have left vestiges and one, a barn, now surrounded by houses, is visible half a block north.

Cortland was the original main stem for this community. When the Bernal Market opened here, ranchers often came down from the hills to buy flour and sugar in 100-pound muslin sacks. Tots from Holly Park went to school in the front room of Thomas Connolly's house on Cortland. Professor George Davidson, who taught them, was delighted when he could move his classes to a two-room shack at number 500, now the site of the Bernal Branch Library. Michael Bogue, a generous man, gave a piece of land a little farther along Cortland at Andover to build a more permanent school, but he didn't do anything about the streets. According to one early record the streets "were so full of ruts and mud, the kids came to school on stilts during the rainy season."

Until the reservoir was built, Holly Park depended on wells and on the flume around the base of Bernal Hill that supplied City Hospital and Pest House, now called San Francisco General Hospital. Walk south on Elsie to reach the reservoir built here by the Spring Valley Water Company in the late 1860's. A caretaker's house stood by it for more than a hundred years, disappearing only recently.

Holly Park circle, technically an oval, interjects beside the reservoir like the neatly barbered dome of some great giant about to burst from the earth. The encircling street was plotted by a German surveyor with the unlikely name of Vitus Wackenreuder. Harvey S. Brown, best known as an attorney for the Southern Pacific Railroad, and his law partner, Pacheco, employed Wackenreuder to lay out streets in Bernal Heights shortly after the War between the States. Many of them had topical names that were later changed. Elsie, for example, was once Cherubuska Street, Winfield was Chapultepec and Moultrie was Minot.

Brown and another co-owner, John F. Cobb, made the city a gift of the seven acres of Holly Park in 1860. The city fathers accepted it ten years later. It took just as long to get around to using the $100,000 voted in 1955 to improve the playground facilities in the park, a vintage firetruck.

Cross to the park to find one walk that encircles and another that cuts it in half like an apple. Take your pick of which you'd rather explore first. The loop looks out on the quaint and modest homes, the firehouse and the housing project which look at the park. The slicer offers, at its crest, an unsurpassed view. As late as 1914 Frank Morton Todd recalls it as an ideal place to see "the extensive truck gardens . . . irrigated by scores of windmills that make a Holland scene." He also pointed out that, "This tract is already being marketed for factory sites, being close to rail and water."

The viewer today will see the results of this marketing, but who will ever see again the windmills or the dairy and truck farms?

A BELL ON THE LAND

Distance: Ten blocks. **Parking:** Fair. **Clothes:** A sweater. **Public Transportation:** Richland bus 9 to Crescent and Murray.

Marooned between the two heedless, ever surging rivers of traffic that are San Jose Avenue and Alemany Boulevard is a pleasant community called St. Mary's Park whose streets have broken out of the restraint of San Francisco's grid pattern to form a bell on the land.

The bell of streets is no accident. It is, in a sense, the blueprint of a bell that rang a hundred years ago in the heart of the Rt. Rev. Joseph Sadoc Alemany, first Catholic Archbishop of San Francisco. It rings today in Moraga, where the fine liberal arts school known as St. Mary's College has removed.

The bishop walked this ground many times. Undoubtedly he followed the Old Spanish Trail from the Mission San Francisco de Asis via Dolores to Mission Street. To avoid the trafficways which have witlessly isolated this community, begin instead at the corner of Murray and Crescent Streets beside St. Mary's playground, once part of St. Mary's College campus.

Look east first and let your mind erase the present. When Alemany first saw it, this was rolling hills, pastures and tidal marshland. It was called the Rancho Rincón de las Salinas y Potrero Viejo, a 4,446 acre grant given to Juan Francisco Bernal for his military service with Anza on the expedition which left Sinaloa, Mexico, to find the bay of St. Francis in 1776. Bernal's grandson, Don Jose Cornelio Bernal, sold part of this grant to Alemany as a site for St. Mary's College in 1850.

At that time the Bernal home stood where St. Luke's Hospital is located and Precita creek ran along what is now Army Street. The 1868 Plat of the Pueblo of San Francisco shows an old stone wall paralleling the creek on the north and dividing the property from Potrero Nuevo, now Potrero Hill. Although they sound like they might have been named yesterday by any real estate dealer, Bernal Heights and Visitacion Valley are shown by these names on the U.S. Coastal Survey map of 1869 which also shows the track of the San Jose railroad along what is now San Jose Avenue.

It was in this bucolic setting that Alemany laid the cornerstone of St. Mary's College in 1862. His diary for July 10, 1863 later records that he had that day blessed the chapel and dedicated St. Mary's College, the needed "school in the far reaches of Mission road."

To find the historical marker placed in commemoration of the founding of the school, walk west on Crescent to Mission where College Avenue joins to form a gore. College is both the clapper and handle of the bell of streets. On the grassy strip at the gore is a pylon with a suggestion of tile roofing, topped by a cross, which tells the story. For twenty-six years, between 1863 and 1889, this was the location of a splendid, much spired four-story brick college building and its equally substantial chapel. To build it, Father James Croke made a two year trek of the Mother Lode country on foot, canvassing prospectors and miners who gave him gold dust and nuggets.

In 1868 Bishop Alemany staffed St. Mary's with seven Christian Brothers, whose order today is as well known for wine as for schools. Justin Drive, the east and south curves of the bell of streets, is named for one of them, Brother Justin, first Christian Brothers president of St. Mary's. Genebern Way, the western curve of the bell, is named for another.

Beyond Mission are two more streets related to the site, St. Mary's Avenue and College Terrace, once faculty homesites. In 1889 the college moved to Oakland, and since 1928, the bells of St. Mary's have rung in Moraga, Contra Costa County, like the echo of a distant time.

FARMERS' MARKET

Walking Time: Allow an hour. **Public Transportation:** Crescent bus 23. **Parking:** Crowded on Saturdays but the turnover is fast. **Clothing:** Warm, but not your best.

Farmers' Market, a city-owned economic safety valve for the diligent handful of people who feed the rest of us, is a sensual, two-block walk that celebrates, week after week, the never ending bounty of this lush land we call California. Despite, or just possibly because of, its half-trapped inaccessibility in a labyrinth of free-ways, it is one of the few places, in an age of the deep-freeze, the squeeze, and the elaborate cold storage, where San Franciscans can benefit directly from bumper crops, or for that matter, tell one season from the next without an almanac.

Autumn, when the pregnant earth traditionally comes to term, is a good season in which to take this walk. A morning in midweek is the best time, for 40,000 hungry people flock into Farmers' Market on a fair Saturday.

Begin this walk at either end of the two ranks of open stalls. In the simplest of systems, farmers' trucks are drawn up in back, customers examine the wares in front. Look down the stalls at the rich nuances of color, salad green, potato brown, citrus golds. As you walk, smell the fruity perfumes of apples, melons, persim-mons, the must of mushrooms, the acrid bouquet of artichokes and bitter melons. Some of these would rot in the fields of the Sacramento and San Joaquin Valleys if it were not for Farmers' Market.

Look for the varieties that seldom appear in shops—ghostly white pumpkins, parti-colored popcorn, Oriental eggplant, Chinese okra, Armenian cucumbers. The 750 farmers who use this public market, one of the few in the United States where there is no mid-dleman, have sixteen different national backgrounds. This rural United Nations comes from 40 California counties (no produce is allowed from out of state) to share with a devoted public their crops for which there is little, and sometimes no demand else-where. Coincidentally, long-time market master Tom Christian, retired, says, "The farmers themselves spend much of their pro-ceeds right here in San Francisco."

Seventy-eight commodities, all fresh fruits, vegetables, nuts, honey or packaged dried fruits, filter through the market in a year to give taxpayers an annual profit of $20,000 on rental of these stalls. In October the walker sees ten kinds of squashes—turban, banana, white, Danish, acorn, butternut, pumpkin and Hubbard—to name but a few.

He will also see the people who sell. Many are men like pioneer pear-seller Joe Sanchetti, or the joking artichoke grower, Ernesto Givanoni, the weather-leathered men that plant, plow and pray over these crops.

Sometimes John Brucato, often called the "Mayor of Farmers' Market," who shepherded it, according to market secretary Lenore

Gray, "from a dream to salvage surplus for wartime use through eighteen stormy years," is among the shoppers. So are housewives who prefer to pay less for smaller-size apples and have more to feed their families. They come from all parts of the city to buy by the bushel, the peck and the lug, for in San Francisco, where the cost of living, like so many things, is second to none, Farmers' Market assures that the old sweet voice of private enterprise is still heard in the land.

McLAREN PARK	**Time:** Allow a morning. **Clothes:** Stout shoes, warm sweater. **Parking:** Plenty. **Public Transportation:** Go via bus 29. (Get off at the last stop on Mansell). Return via bus 52 from the corner of Prague and Brazil.

There is a walk in San Francisco for the saint, the poet, the sage, and for all who cannot get out of their minds the rueful lines in E. M. Forster's *Abinger Harvest:* "You can make a town, you can make a desert, you can even make a garden; but you can never, never make the country, because it was made by Time."

San Francisco's country walk lies within John McLaren Park. If you would walk the country road meandering through rocky grassland, windbreak lanes, along a lofty ridge, go some sunny morning to the corner of Mansell and Bowdoin Streets. On the one hand, just beyond the new junior high school recently constructed, there is a greenhouse. On the other, a farmhouse. Below, in any direction, one can see the city-dynamic, industry whittling at residential areas, houses biting into land that was grassy pasture within the memory of a ten-year-old boy and freeways writhing monstrous and unseeing through it all.

Turn west, away from what Man has made. Direct your feet along the ridge John McLaren loved. At University and Mansell, the boulevard makes a sharp transition from cement to red-rock road. Last year another greenhouse stood here whose wooden water tower no longer shoulders the sky. In a few steps you pass from a shabby corner where the brambles grow to open land.

Follow the road past the foundations of an old horse ranch, traceable in forgotten masonry, and a tree-lined lane to nowhere. Like the Spaniards who once pastured cattle from Mission Dolores here, like Jacob Leese, who was granted the Canada de Guadalupe y Rodeo Viejo y Visitación and traded it off to Robert Ridley, another pioneer, the horses, hostlers, riders and ranchers are written on the wind.

Off north, the walker reaches a pond, horsemen's stables, an outdoor amphitheatre and evidence that that curse of the land, the off road vehicle, has raped its way over hills and lawns, making inroads that may lead to erosion-canyons.

Follow the cobble-curbed broad road and soon the Cow Palace is visible south, squatting like Gulliver among Lilliputian houses. Sharply below lies McLaren Park golf course, a goat pasture any Scot would feel at home on. Beyond is McLaren swimming pool and Hahn playground. At the next turn, they are out of sight and shortly the walker reaches a three-tined fork in the road. The middle way leads up to a hill surmounted by a bullet-pocked, graffiti-scratched water tank, bold as a Bufano statue. The low road leads through a valley. Bear left along the main road to end near transportation and the Luther Burbank School at La Grand and Brazil.

What else is there to see? Gophers and groves of trees. Rocks to throw. Grass, leaves, twigs and the contours of this old concretion we call the earth. The moods and mysteries of the living land. The sound of surging tides in spring. The dry whispering drift of dead leaves in the fall. Trees laid open like a shattered door. The spider's web, dew-flecked, unbroken. The vision of what the West offered its pioneers. And if you look deeply enough, along this little-traveled way, your own heart, city scarred.

OCEAN

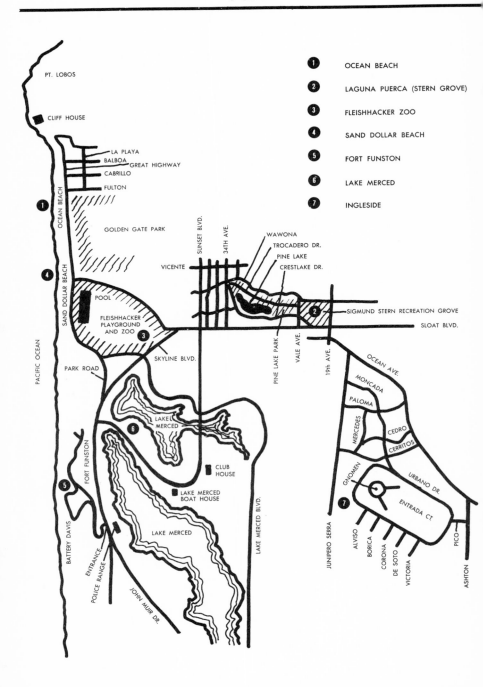

1 OCEAN BEACH

2 LAGUNA PUERCA (STERN GROVE)

3 FLEISHHACKER ZOO

4 SAND DOLLAR BEACH

5 FORT FUNSTON

6 LAKE MERCED

7 INGLESIDE

PT. LOBOS

CLIFF HOUSE

LA PLAYA
BALBOA
GREAT HIGHWAY
CABRILLO
FULTON

OCEAN BEACH

GOLDEN GATE PARK

SUNSET BLVD.
34TH AVE.
WAWONA
TROCADERO DR.
PINE LAKE
CRESTLAKE DR.

VICENTE

POOL

FLEISHHACKER
PLAYGROUND
AND ZOO

SAND DOLLAR BEACH

PACIFIC OCEAN

SIGMUND STERN RECREATION GROVE
SLOAT BLVD.

SKYLINE BLVD.

PINE LAKE PARK
VALE AVE.
19th AVE.

OCEAN AVE.
MONCADA
PALOMA
MERCEDES
CEDRO
CERRITOS
URBANO DR.

PARK ROAD

LAKE
MERCED

LAKE MERCED BLVD.

CLUB
HOUSE

LAKE MERCED
BOAT HOUSE

FORT FUNSTON

GNOMEN
ENTRADA CT.

LAKE MERCED

JUNIPERO SERRA

ALVISO
BORICA
CORONA
DE SOTO
VICTORIA
PICO
ASHTON

BATTERY DAVIS

ENTRANCE
POLICE RANGE

JOHN MUIR DR.

OCEAN BEACH

Distance: 3 miles. **Time:** Allow half a day. **Clothes:** Sandals for beachwalking. **Parking:** Good. **Transportation:** Muni cars 2x, 2, 18, 5 and 38 to go. 18 or L to return.

Three miles of the great primordial heat engine that is the Pacific Ocean wash and warm San Francisco along a bare selvedge we call Ocean Beach. The footprints of Palou, Moncada, Kipling, Stevenson, Sam Brannan, President McKinley, Bertie the Birdman, Adolph Sutro and Actress Adah Isaacs Menken have all been smoothed from this beach by the "dilute solution of everything" the Indians called the "Sundown Sea." The straight sand strand is a clean strip of the continental shelf, but to the perceptive man of inquiring mind, this three miles of inner space is the most mysterious, stimulating, refreshing and challenging walk in the city.

Here the future lies, not ahead, as comedian Mort Sahl would have it, but squishing through one's bare toes. The sea "will ultimately determine conditions of life in the rest of the world," the late President John F. Kennedy once told Congress. He may have been thinking of "aquaculture," the collection of sciences already transforming fishermen from hunters to farmers, miners from prospectors to chemists, and skindivers from hobby-swimmers to explorers. He may also have been thinking, as the walker will, of how little we know about the ocean, a frontier whose resources are as yet uncounted, whose topography has yet to be plumbed, whose climates are unguessed and whose secrets hold the key to mankind's origin and possibly his survival.

"The amorous waves pout up their moist lips to the kisses of the wooer," wrote Frank Soulé in *The Annals of San Francisco*. In his day, 1850, the ambitious walker who went out to the ocean would have found little else than waves, jetsam, driftwood, scuttling crabs, sand fleas and bull kelp on the beach, and the Farallones in the distance. The sea lions on Arch Rock, Hermit Rock, Cone Rock, Repose Rock and North Seal Rock, as the islands below Cliff House are named, were occasionally disturbed by high-wire artists.

Cliff House, the fifth building to bear this name on this site, is a logical place to begin walking Ocean Beach, for it stands on an

eminence. From it the walker who can resist the Camera Oscura, the totem poles and the gypcracks, will find the whole beach laid out below him like a magnificent broadloom fringed by the manes of Poseidon's stallions. Long ago at the south end of the beach, another famous inn, Ocean House, offered refreshments to those who drove along the sand for sport, or to watch the races at nearby Ocean House race course. Now Fleishhacker Zoo and Fort Funston are the landmarks, with Point Montara lying blue in the spindrift beyond.

Playland-at-the-Beach, an amusement park known for its transitory thrills, hotdogs, enchiladas and rifle ranges, replaced the Golden Gate Ostrich Farm which was located on the sand dunes here when plumed hoods were in feather. The walker who clings to the paved esplanade can also see the great Dutch windmills of Golden Gate Park, and a beach chalet. Robert's by the Sea, once the favorite dining place of the horseracing crowd that frequented Ingleside race course, is now gone.

For those who are unafraid of returning to the primitive prelude of our civilization, there is escape from the world down on the sand. Here the walker will see not only the Farallones, 25 miles offshore, on a fair day, but sometimes murres, petrels, cormorants, sandpipers and albatross. Children, artists for a moment, draw in the clean wetness, dance in the shallow withdrawing wave, or run, because they like it, on the broad bright sand. Some of the children are old enough to vote.

SIGMUND STERN MEMORIAL GROVE

Distance: About a mile. **Clothes:** Flat shoes, sweater. **Parking:** Good except on concert days. **Public Transportation:** Nineteenth Ave. bus 28 or Sloat bus 18.

Let it be close to two o'clock on a sunny summer Sunday afternoon in San Francisco. Let warm trade winds fill the green canvas sign saying, "Concert Today" until it billows like a full sail in the trees. Let the chains barring car traffic festoon the grand entrance at Nineteenth Avenue and Sloat Boulevard. Let a happy throng, burbling with anticipatory excitement at hearing Jan Peerce or Arthur Fiedler, flow like an eager river down through the stately eucalyptus trees.

Then, for music lovers, there is no other walk in the City to compare with a stroll down the gully we call Stern Grove. The Sunday song sample is apt to whet the appetite for further exploration of the Grove among those music lovers who are also walkers. If you have never rambled through the unusual terrain of this acoustically remarkable arroyo, pack a picnic supper some evening when daylight saving time is with us and go to Stern Grove. Begin your walk at Wawona and Twenty-first Avenue. Follow the broad path through the western end of a neatly clipped lawn. The long low building on the lawn is a lath house. The more permanent one beyond it, near two shrub-shrouded lawn bowling greens, is Wawona clubhouse. One walker recently enjoyed observing, through a large picture window, the Balkan Dance Club taking a lesson in Greek folk dancing from Anna Efstathiou.

The footpath that approaches the clubhouse also leads to the grand entrance of the Grove in time, but this is the long way round. Look instead for the red rock path behind the green shingled maintenance shed, one of the two at the edge of the trees. Follow this trail, which has almost as many switchbacks as the winding block of Lombard Street, down into the canyon floor.

Surprisingly, it soon reveals an open meadow, a lily pond and a series of outdoor picnic rooms, each complete with barbecue pits and tables. At trail's end, newly painted a subtle yellow, frosted in white carpenter's lace, is the quaint Victorian building that was once a notorious roadhouse, the Trocadero Inn, built in 1892 by George W. Greene, Jr., scion of a Maine family who homesteaded this land in 1847.

The saga of the Troc reads like a libretto by Zane Grey and includes gun battles to hold a tin-lined fort against landgrabbers, an impromptu duel over the charms of a Spanish senorita, and raids seeking the leaders of a corrupt political ring. Look for the two bulletholes that still adorn the main doors on the broad vine-shaped veranda next to the doors which lead to the former barroom. Community groups now use the Troc as a meeting place.

Three trails lead up the north wall of the canyon. Another, across the grassy lawn of the amphitheatre, follows a stream past dressing rooms to the stage. Unless a practice performance is in session, there is nothing to prevent a would-be Barber of Seville from trying his voice on Figaro with the wind in the treetops for accompaniment. If it is about sundown, Mrs. Alexandra Alexander, a music lover who lives nearby, and her great white Pyrenees, Russland, may come by.

PINE LAKE

Parking: Some at the park terminus of Vale Avenue. **Clothes:** Comfortable shoes. Sweater. **Public Transportation:** 28 Nineteenth Avenue bus or 18 Sloat bus. **Distance:** About a mile to loop the lake and return to Sloat and Nineteenth.

The Sunset, like every district of San Francisco, has its secret places of special enchantment. The cupped hand of land which cradles spring-fed Laguna Puerca, or as we now call it, Pine Lake, is one of these.

Part of the gorge known since 1932 as Sigmund Stern Memorial Grove, and a second gift to the city from the gracious woman whose husband the grove commemorates, Pine Lake is bordered by Crestlake and Wawona Streets and is most easily approached by Vale Avenue. Walkers who have found the route return again and again for a quiet, soul-restoring interlude.

When the arias of the summer music festival are stilled, loons call here, and owls. Mallards nest in the tule rushes. Canvasbacks sun, seldom disturbed, in the grassy meadows. Rather than pines, the trees that sigh on the slopes, shutting out the clangor of the surrounding city, are eucalypti imported from Australia by pioneer George W. Greene, Jr., whose father homesteaded this land.

It has not always been so peaceful. Two of the city's liveliest gun battles rattled down this acoustically unique canyon. In each the white hats ultimately prevailed, the baddies got what is known as "justice." The first was a landgrab in which one David Mahoney

tried to snooker the Greene family by some cagey legal shenani-
gans. The Greenes, in heroic frontier tradition, built themselves a
metal-lined fort and held it for three months under siege against
hired "redshirts." They held the fort, Greene Senior said later, by
shooting "low, in the stomach, for it would take two men to carry
them away." A special act of Congress in 1887 reinstated their
grant on the land they had farmed for forty years.

Abe Ruef, brains of the corrupt Ruef-Schmidt regime, *circa*
1906, was a target, if not the hero of the second gunfight. Bullet
holes in the door of the Hansel-and-Gretel style inn, once a resort
known as the Trocadero, are souvenirs of a fight reputed to have
driven Ruef into hiding under the eaves. Despite any discomforts,
his sojourn was undoubtedly pleasanter than a subsequent one at
San Quentin.

There are also some bullet holes in the stairs of the lodge, recently renovated after a vandal-set fire. They are supposed to date
from 1892, when the elite, C. A. Hooper, Adolph Spreckels and
North Pole explorer Dr. Frederick Cook among them, frequented
the "Troc." One of their contemporaries was quick on the trigger
and jealous of a Spanish señorita.

Hiram Cook, a prize-fight referee, leased the property during
its heyday as a roadhouse. Sportsmen fished Pine Lake for trout
by day, lovers rowed on it at twilight and danced nearby in a
pavilion hung with paper lanterns by night.

Native son Peter Tamony, 2876 Twenty-fourth Street, can re-
cal going to "moonlight picnics" there via trolley on the Market
Street railway in a specially designed, heavily-curtained charter car.
"It was basically a funeral car," he says, "and was used to transport
whole funeral parties, including casket, to the cemeteries in far
San Mateo County." Other times it rang with noisy merrymakers.

Pagliacci, Traviata, La Bohème, Iolanthe and *Pinafore* ring
forth instead in our time. Pine Lake amplifies their notes in season.
Out of it, Superintendent Cliff Robinson and his crew of gardeners
create a stage-setting Verdi, Leoncavallo, Puccini and Gilbert and
Sullivan would find unbelievable, and the public, grateful to Mrs.
Sigmund Stern, finds delightful.

INGLESIDE

Distance: Half a mile. **Walking Time:** Allow an hour to watch the sundial shadow. **Parking:** Good. **Clothes:** Citified. **Public Transportation:** Ingleside car K through Twin Peaks tunnel or 17 and 28 buses.

What may well be, as its creator claimed, "the largest and most magnificent sundial in the world" is one of San Francisco's pleasant, if seldom-touted, curiosities. It is also an informal monument to the Twin Peaks tunnel, to the Panama Canal, to the sport of kings, and coincidentally, to the garden ovals and crescents of Bloomsbury, London. Beyond all this, it is well worth a discovery trip for the walker who enjoys a goal or climax for his excursions.

To find it, go to the southwestern section of the city and look for the wide stone gates proclaiming Ingleside Terrace. There are several along Ocean Avenue and along Junipero Serra Boulevard near the point where these two thoroughfares converge. Moncada Way is the key street for those who enter from Junipero Serra. Paloma Avenue, off Ocean, soon meets Moncada. Follow Moncada to Urbano Drive, a street that overlays exactly the one-mile loop that was once Ingleside Race Track.

As you wind past the gracious houses along Moncada, imagine this quiet street instead as it must have been when Ingleside Race Track opened, Thanksgiving Day, November 28, 1885, crowded with toffs, hoarse-voiced bookies, candy butchers, sportsmen, gamblers, the fashionable and the curious. The clubhouse stood at what is now the corner of Moncada and Cerritos Avenue. The bandstand was at Moncada and Urbano. A. B. Spreckels, Henry J. Crocker, Ed Corrigan and O. B. MacDonough had started the Pacific Coast Jockey Club in direct competition with Thomas Williams of Bay District Track and his California Jockey Club.

According to *Breeder and Sportsman,* the *Sports Illustrated* of its time, James F. (Polo Jim) Caldwell had been hired as starter at a salary "comparable to that of the President of the United States." Despite threatening rain, excitement ran high. Eight thousand people came out for the day, many grumbling because the trains couldn't handle the crowds, and a horse named Semper Lex won the first race. December 31, 1905 was the last time racing hooves and silk-clad jockeys flashed around Ingleside track.

Walk east on Urbano to Borica, then south a few steps on Borica to reach Entrada Court, a V-shaped street with a circular park at its point. There, in the center of the little park, often swarming with children, is the great slanting 26-foot high gnomon, or shaft, of the sundial. Once the dial, bordered with great Roman numerals, had a reflecting pool in its face, formal flower beds marking the major compass points on the surrounding grass and four columns representing childhood, youth, manhood and old age, for embellishment. This elaborate architectural confection was dedicated in 1915 with dancing in the street, nymphs in costume and live storks pulling baby buggies. Its story began when the Urban Realty Improvement Company purchased the 148 acres of Ingleside Race Track property and hired civil engineer J. M. Morser to plan a residence park. Morser was inspired by Bloomsbury, an area many planners today acknowledge may be unsurpassed for urban livability and human scale.

"Just why the final blast at Panama that permitted the waters of the Atlantic and the Pacific to intermingle should occur on the same day that the sundial at Ingleside was dedicated may not at first be apparent," says a commemorative booklet belonging to Mrs. N. N. Presson of 70 Cerritos Avenue, "but the 'kiss of the oceans' promise of the coming greatness of San Francisco needed as a complement some assurance of the fitting homes required for its happiness and highest welfare."

On its back cover, around a fanciful medal of the kiss, the booklet proclaims, "The Panama Canal unites the Atlantic and the Pacific. The Twin Peaks Tunnel unites San Francisco and Ingleside Terrace."

Mrs. W. B. Wheldon, 485 Marina Boulevard, whose father, R. D. McElroy, had been a member of the Urban Realty Company, can recall sliding down the sundial gnomon as a child. Children still slide down it today with the blessing of the Ingleside Terrace Association, which maintains the park.

LAKE MERCED

Clothes: Walking shoes and coat. **Time:** Best in the morning before fog comes in. **Distance:** A mile and a half in this lap. **Parking:** Fair. **Public Transportation:** Bus 72.

In the southwesternmost corner of San Francisco, where the San Andreas fault slides into the sea, encroached on by slurbs and poached on by ever-widening roads, there lies, in a drowned river valley surrounded by dunes, a remarkable V-shaped lake. Our forebears might well have called it miraculous for within recorded time is has contained both salt water and fresh. The switchover happened between 1869 and 1895, according to Dr. R. C. Miller of the Academy of Sciences. Today small fishy animals of both persuasions live in the spring-fed lake, happy, presumably, as clams.

Since it is the early birds that get the word, among other things, it was the Spaniards who named the lake. They called it Laguna de Nuestra Señora de la Merced, the Lake of our Lady of Mercy. Lake Merced, the verbal vestige to which we have clung, like the lake itself, is a good bit smaller than it once was. At present it is 30 feet deep, has 386 acres under water and is a standby reservoir for the city. For 43 years it supplied us with 3.1 million gallons of drinking water daily. Now it supplies sprinkling water for golf greens, and fun for fishermen who call it the city's "back-yard fishin' hole." It might also be called the place where a fault becomes a virtue.

As a sample of the many good walks around Lake Merced, go some sunny morning to the end of Sunset Boulevard where it crosses Lake Merced Boulevard. Beyond a parking circle, the walker will find a broad red-rock path. Follow it across a foot-bridge, one of the few remaining in the city, which offers a mid-point of inspection for the north flange of the lake, and a place to linger, dream and muse. When the mystery of water reflection wearies, follow the footpath uphill. It emerges in Harding Park, an 18-hole golf course open to the public, behind the restaurant. Walk around in front of the clubhouse to continue on the road which leads westerly between the two flanges of the lake. At the first turn of the road, look to your right to see one of the few remaining marshy arroyos where migrating waterfowl can find food and shelter. Marine biologists can also find the *Relict Fauna of Lake Merced* as reported in 1958 by Dr. Miller. Rowboats are moored in the next inlet.

The Lake Merced boat house, completed in 1959 by the Recreation and Park Department, is the next building one encounters. The nearby bar and restaurant is leased as a concession to Aurie Kuntz, who once operated this fringe of the lake as a private playground. Small sailboats are for rent and there is a children's pier below the boathouse. Across the road is a barbecue area and a model race car track. On Skyline Boulevard, bear north, toward the Fleishhacker Zoo on the footpath between the freeway and the lake until you reach Lake Merced Boulevard. Along this perimeter, Dr. Robert T. Orr and his wife, Dorothy, co-authors of *Common Fungi of the San Francisco Bay Region,* have found some of the best mushroom hunting in the city. Blewits, the purple mushroom known to scientists as *Tricholoma personata,* and the wrinkled, prune-like *Helvella lacunosa,* are common here.

If this mile and a half jaunt, which ends where the walk began, hasn't tired you, there are other pleasures worth seeking at Lake Merced. Historians can see where Rivera y Moncada camped in 1774, or with persistence discover the approximate site of the last duel-to-death in San Francisco. Two obelisk-shaped markers and a tablet mark the little dell in which Senator David Broderick was fatally wounded by Judge David Terry. The entrance path is off Lakeview Drive and El Portal Way.

Engineers will find, at 17 feet above sea level on the site of the Spring Valley pumping station, a new pumphouse that lifts water in a 105 foot rise from Crystal Springs at 280 feet to Sunset Reservoir. They will also find a watermain that crosses a lake, the causeway that is a favorite with bank-fishermen.

FLEISHHACKER ZOO

Walking Time: Allow half a day. **Clothes:** Take a sweater. **Parking:** Fair. **Public Transportation:** L streetcar or Sloat bus 18.

Fleishhacker Zoo, one of the most entertaining walks in San Francisco, has about 600 resident animals and a sense of humor.

For example, the saigas, rare big-nosed Russian goats, were described on arrival as "nervous, hard to get along with, ugly and difficult to keep alive in captivity," by former Director Carey Baldwin, once a resident. Unlike the hero of David Garnett's *Man in the Zoo,* Director Baldwin did not live in a cage, but in a cottage, as he describes it, "in the out-back."

Baldwin has also described a gibbon as "whooping it up like a discontented mother-in-law." His reason for not getting a mate for Percy, the mandrill, is that "this is one species whose amorous activities are so human they are likely to unhinge visitors at the zoo."

Visitors at the zoo number about two million a year and are usually unfeathered bipeds, although a pelican, an egret and raccoon have come to call, seeking a home. Many of the visitors are members of the nonprofit San Francisco Zoological Society, a business-like bunch of buffs whose president is Allan Fleishhacker, son of the man who started the zoo in 1929. The society runs concessions to raise money to purchase rare animals and shares the sanguine "zoo attitude." When keepers wrested a would-be suicide off the guard-rail of the lion grotto, the society's newsletter congratulated them for alertness by saying, "It shows to what lengths the keepers will go in order to keep their charges from dining on unauthorized items."

Once a steel door on the gorilla cage banged down on the head of Mr. Carroll Soo-hoo, best-known local zoo fan. Another Soo-hoo might have said "Boo-hoo." Not Carroll. As blood ran in his eyes and Director Baldwin rushed him off to the hospital, Mr. Soo-hoo commented, "Isn't it amazing what the human skull can stand."

The walker who strolls through the 30 acres bounded by Great Highway, Sloat, Sunset and Skyline Boulevards, will see humor in action if he looks for it. The quadrupeds may not be performing, but the bipeds always are. In a relaxed atmosphere, he will also see the aoudad, cheetah, coatimundi, cassowary, emu, cockatoo, kangaroo, wallaroo, nilgai, tapir, lesser panda, yak and a peccary affectionately known as Gregory. He will also see lions, roaring tigers, enormous camels, relevant elephants and the preposterous rhinoceros, an unbelievable animal which one recent playwright, Ionesco, thinks contemporary man is turning into.

Begin this walk at the Forty-fifth Avenue gate on Sloat, to the tune of "Carnival of Animals" if you remember it. Walk south, past Mother's House, like Fleishhacker pool built in 1922 on land acquired from the Spring Valley Water Company. Pass picnic tables, Storyland, playground, vintage locomotive, carousel, miniature steam train and the new Children's Zoo. Ultimately you reach a turnstile. Go through it. There are no chained bears. San Francisco's first zoo, operated in 1856 in a basement at Clay and Leidesdorff Streets by grizzly hunter James Capen Adams, had chained bears. The San Francisco Zoo not only dislikes chains, it would prefer that all enclosures be barless. Forty-two acres of Fort Funston will soon be developed to give hoofed animals more unfenced home on the range. This land replaces zoo acreage swapped away by the city to developers twenty years ago.

Near the turnstile is a kiosk to purchase "zoo keys," tickets for the "elephant train," gimcracks called "giftus extraordinaire," soda pop and such. There is also a map. First-time visitors can use Monkey Island, a moated enclosure, and the mall where the elephants, May, Virge and Babe (named for the Fleishhacker children) parade, for landmarks.

Like Aristotle, the first zoologist, walkers will find they can learn about people from zoo animals. The llama, for example, spits when he is miffed. Like many small boys, when he doesn't get his own way, he throws up. One zoo fan is looking forward to the day when he finds a tot and a llama performing within range of his camera lens on the same instant.

FORT
FUNSTON

Walking Time: Allow two hours.
Distance: Roads within Fort Fun-
ston cover about a mile and a half.
Walkers should stick to them. There
are sump holes and barbed wire
around the bunkers. **Parking:** Best
place is near the zoo where Sloat
Boulevard ends at Great Highway.
Public Transportation: L Taraval
streetcar or 18 Sloat bust to zoo.
Clothes: Boots or stout shoes.
Warm jacket.

Fort Funston, the last undeveloped, uncrowded and unspoiled
chunk of sea-coastal headland left in San Francisco, is a narrow,
116 acre strip of beautiful moonscape dunes which lies south of
Fleishhacker Zoo. It is also the dike, 1300 feet wide, which
holds back the Pacific Ocean from resalting Lake Merced, the
terminal lake in a freshwater chain whose links sparkle along
that prominent rift valley known as the San Andreas fault.

Most of its three-fourths of a mile frontage on Skyline Boulevard
is 30 feet above the highway, a geological advantage which creates
the illusion of remoteness most of us seek when we go on vacation.
Up in the looney, windcarved, lunar dunes of Fort Funston, the
advancing urban sprawl nearby, with all its pressures and congestion, seems farther away than Los Angeles.

When troops of the Spanish-American War camped on this
land in 1898, it was called Laguna Merced Military Reservation.
The records don't show whether anyone thought it droll in 1917
that a fort situated on a seismologically tender ledge should be
renamed for Major General Frederick Funston whose troops
policed San Francisco after the 1906 Quake and Shake.

Much of the time Fort Funston, a suitably difficult practice
place for "war game" landing, has been inaccessible to the public.
Since 1961 walkers have had the privilege of exploring the gullies,
bluffs and bunkers of this rugged terrain. The Golden Gate National Recreation Area includes Fort Funston, a natural public
park.

Highest point on the grounds is Battery Davis, a tremendous
underground gun emplacement built in 1939 and obsolete all too

soon, which stands about 200 feet above sea level. Southbound motorists on Great Highway will recognize Battery Davis as the truncated pyramid they see silhouetted like a flat hat against the sky beyond Sloat Boulevard. Skyline Boulevard is destined to straighten out, more parking will be provided and the zoo will be extended at the north end of Fort Funston.

Enter either from the parking area south of the zoo or from Skyline at the gate across from the San Francisco Police Pistol Range on the shore of Lake Merced. On arrival at Battery Davis, visitors will be surprised to find that it is a long dark tunnel. In one of the plans for use of this property prepared by the Department of City Planning it was suggested that "with a minimum of reconditioning an ideal record storage center could be maintained here by the city." It would also make a bomb shelter no gloomier than most.

Between the bunker and the sea is a warm sheltered promontory, one of several excellent locations for campsites or picnicking. From the top of the bunker, enterprising climbers will see the striking vista of Lake Merced, the westering city neighborhoods and Twin Peaks in the distance. A scant 20 years ago much of this land was still the Sutro Forest of eucalyptus or rolling dunes covered with beach grass, lupine, sea asters, sand verbena, sage and scarlet paint brush. Many of these flowers persist in breaking through the sea-fig ground cover of Fort Funston. From the promontory walkers will also see the Pacific, the foundations of a burned gun-club, an old ammunition dump, two roads, other hidden bunkers and possibly albatross. The underlying Merced formation of the Pliocene, whose crack is one of the classic geological lessons, has given this land a shaky past, but its future, tremors notwithstanding, is recreational. It is now part of the G.G.N.R.A.

SAND DOLLAR BEACH

Walking Time: Two hours. **Distance:** Two miles each way. **Nearby Public Transportation:** L car to the zoo. **Parking:** Great on weekdays. **Clothes:** Sandals, shorts and a warm jacket. Take a burlap bag for fossil collecting.

"Well, I'll tell you what happened to me at Fleishhacker Zoo the other day," sings Bob Helm in an old Turk Murphy comic number called "Evolution Mama," whose topical lyrics date back to that paleontological highwater mark, the Scopes trial.

In the song someone makes a monkey out of the shouter by shaking his family tree. At Fleishhacker, Turk, Helm and the lyricist were closer than they dreamed to an evolutionary revelation. Some 200 yards west, across Ocean Highway, about a smooth round stone's throw along the sand, there is something to shout about. It is a smooth round stone, gray and white and wave-worn into the flat shape best for "skipping the waves" in one of childhood's oldest games.

Ocean Beach, south of Sloat, is where *Anorthoscutum interlineatum Stimpson,* an extinct sand dollar, washes out of the Merced formation from a V-shaped fossil bed of the Pliocene epoch which lies offshore. Like flotwood and driftsam on beaches everywhere, this sea treasure is most easily found by the man on foot.

The walk along Ocean Beach, San Francisco's frontier of the chuckling sea, may be cold, but as surfcasters, skindivers, sandpipers and psychiatrists could tell you, it has its own exhilarating attractions. Among them are the spindrift, the striped bass, an infinity of horizon and the percussive rhythm of amniotic sea on sand.

For rockhounds and anyone else who admits to that primitive urge to "get something for nothing" which we sometimes call beachcombing, the portion of beach which lies below Fort Funston and the Olympic Club's Oceanside course has all these things plus an extra dimension—the quality of the quest. The fossil sand dollars here are many, but erosion, the most impartial of forces, produces few that are pristine. The walker who finds a perfect specimen may consider himself lucky.

"Nutcracker Man," recently discovered, might have found *Anorthoscutum* on Ocean Beach if he had walked there, just as the stroller may today, for this fossil sand dollar had been around from one to eight million years before Man made it out of the primordial ooze to the beaches of Planet Earth.

Certainly the Indians who loved the Sundown Sea must have marveled at the rock whose pattern has petals, and quite possibly Jose Antonio Galindo, Francisco de Haro and Francisco Guerrero y Palomares, all of whom owned Rancho Laguna de la Merced at one time or another, must have puzzled over it. It was not until 1856 that the fossil was described and identified, scientifically.

Many of us today would pass the unique sea-loot with barely a glance. Not so the bright-eyed young ladies whom walkers may find lugging a burlap bag along the beach after a storm. These student geologists, in all probability, will be senior Girl Scouts, scouting up fossils to "swap" with girls from all over the world at the international roundup held by their organization every three years.

One group looking for fossils included Eda Carlson and her older sister Rowena, who was president of the San Francisco intertroop council. Rowena took fossil sand dollars to the roundup at Colorado Springs in 1959. They've been in demand ever since. She says, "A good 'swap' should be educational or decorative and must be something that can't be duplicated elsewhere."

With her were Scouts Ellen and Erin McGinty, one of whom chimed in, "And it should be something your mother won't pitch out as junk when you bring it home."

Anorthoscutum fills all these requirements nobly. It also makes a good paperweight. For the walker who doesn't find one, the exuberant, everliving sea offers a consolation prize. This is *Dendraster excentricus Escholtz.,* also a sand dollar but not extinct. It is a fit subject to contemplate, in this trigger-tender age of atomic peril, while singing, "Evolution, mama, don't you make a monkey out of me."

INDEX